BERLITZ®

CANADA

How to use our guide

These 256 pages cover the **highlights of Canada,** grouped into six regions. Although not exhaustive, our selection of sights will enable you to make the best of your trip.

The **sights** to see are contained between pages 47 and 195. Those most highly recommended are pinpointed by the Berlitz traveller symbol.

The **Where to Go** section on page 43 will help you plan your visit according to the time available.

For **general background** see the sections Canada and the Canadians (p. 8), History (p. 16), Facts and Figures (p. 28), and Native Peoples (p. 34).

Entertainment and **activities** (including eating out) are described between pages 196 and 217.

The **practical information,** hints and tips you will need before and during your trip begin on page 218. This section is arranged alphabetically with a list for easy reference.

The **map section** at the back of the book (pp. 239–251) will help you find your way around and locate the principal sights.

Finally, if there is anything you cannot find, look in the complete **index** (pp. 252–256).

6th edition
Reprinted with corrections 1996

CONTENTS

CONTENTS

Cover photo: Rafting on the Chilliwack River.

Text:	Jack Altman
Staff Editor:	Barbara Ender
Layout:	Doris Haldemann
Photography:	cover, pp. 8, 11, 13, 15, 18, 21, 32, 97, 149, 152, 159, 160, 163, 165, 180, 186, 205, 209, 211, 217 Jürg Donatsch; pp. 50, 55, 58, 61, 64, 69, 75, 80 Erling Mandelmann; pp. 87, 90, 93, 96, 100, 101, 106, 112, 113 Ted Grant; pp. 9, 154, 198 Province of British Columbia; pp. 25, 119, 121, 125, 130 Nova Scotia Tourism; p. 41 Ministry of Tourism and Recreation, Ontario; pp. 35, 193, 194 Government of the Northwest Territories; pp. 183, 202 Saskatchewan Tourism; pp. 45, 172, 175, 177, 201 Alberta Tourism; pp. 109, 114 Ministère du Tourisme, Québec; pp. 134, 213 Prince Edward Island Tourism; p. 137 Tourism New Brunswick; pp. 141, 143 Government of Newfoundland and Labrador; p. 191 Yukon Government Photo; p. 206 Manitoba Tourism; p. 78 National Gallery of Canada, Ottawa; p. 168 Tourism Canada Photo.
Cartography:	🗺 Falk-Verlag, Hamburg

Acknowledgements
We would like to express our thanks to Georgia Maclean of the Canadian High Commission in London, the heads of all the provincial tourist offices in Canada, as well as Canadian International Airlines, for their assistance in the preparation of this guide. We are also grateful to Alice Taucher for invaluable help. A special note of thanks for Gerry Altman's fraternal guidance on the west coast.

Found an error or an omission in this Berlitz Guide? Or a change or new feature we should know about? Our editor would be happy to hear from you, and a postcard would do.

Although we make every effort to ensure the accuracy of all the information in this book, changes occur incessantly. We cannot therefore take responsibility for facts, prices, addresses and circumstances in general that are constantly subject to alteration.

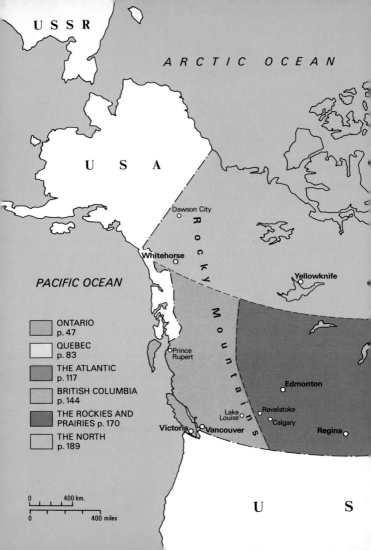

USSR

ARCTIC OCEAN

U S A

PACIFIC OCEAN

Dawson City

Whitehorse

R
o
c
k
y

Yellowknife

M
o
u
n
t
a
i
n
s

Prince
Rupert

Edmonton

Lake
Louise

Revelstoke

Calgary

Regina

Victoria

Vancouver

0   400 km.

0   400 miles

U   S

CANADA AND THE CANADIANS

The land is immense. It crowns the North American continent with an intriguing combination of sophisticated urban living and indomitable wilderness. The advanced industrial society that stretches along the border with the United States looks out of its back door onto inexhaustible forests, a powerful network of rivers and lakes, and mountain ranges reaching up into the Arctic tundra.

To those with only a dim notion of the place, Canada is a land of year-round snows, of polar bears and Eskimos, of ear-muffed lumberjacks huddled around a campfire with an Arctic wolf howling in the distance.

American tourists still drive over the border in July with skis on the car roof. They'd have a long way to go before they found any snow. Yet the Arctic image persists—gold-hungry Charlie Chaplin eating his boots in the Yukon with a blizzard blowing outside.

For most Canadians, the Far North starts beyond the tree-line in their most populous prov-inces, Quebec and Ontario. This is the beginning of the great gla-cial plateau known as the Can-adian Shield, stretching in a wide arc along the shores of the Hudson Bay, across northern Manitoba and Saskatchewan to the Northwest Territories. The

Spanning a vast continent from the fishing villages of Nova Scotia to the snowy peaks of British Columbia.

terrain is rough and rocky, strewn with swamps and lakes as far as the bleak tundra. Beyond that, the vast, unyielding permafrost of the Arctic, where a national park on Baffin Island says it all: *Auyuittuq*, the place that never melts. But under the ice, there's gold, silver, lead, tungsten, uranium, oil and gas, with Indians and Eskimos (who prefer to be called Inuit) vying for control of these riches with the federal government.

The cities make a seductive launching pad for tackling the great outdoors. Beside the sleek limousine in the suburban driveway, as likely as not, you'll also find a canoe.

Montreal epitomizes Canada's special mélange of New World modernity and Old World charm: massive new skyscrapers and gracious red-brick mansions. For many North Americans, the unashamed quaintness of old Quebec City offers a first taste of things French. Similarly, bouncing boomtown Toronto offers Europeans a gleaming Canadian version of America, "cleaner and nicer," say the immodest locals—and many Americans, too. Federal capital Ottawa is more attractive for its national museums than its major "industry", government bureaucracy. If the disarming brashness of Calgary reminds many of Texas, the scintillating location between

the Pacific Ocean and the mountains gives Vancouver a relaxed elegance all its own.

Beyond the cities, Canada still talks a pioneering language: challenge, high risk, adventure, remote frontiers to chart, empty wastelands yet to conquer. In the whole world, there is no country bigger than Canada. Its landmass could swallow the United States, with France, Belgium and the Netherlands thrown in. The

forests alone cover an area six times the size of France. But the population is ten times smaller than that of its American neighbour. And the majority know very little about the rest of their country. It's all too far away.

The railways and roads that make it physically possible to get across this giant country have been vital symbolic instruments of national unity: in the 19th century the transcontinental Ca-

The country's ethnic mix goes way beyond the simple division of Anglo- and French-Canadians.

nadian Pacific Railway, then the Canadian National, and now the Trans-Canada Highway, which enables you to drive from the Atlantic to the Pacific Ocean without stopping at a traffic light.

In the east, tough, stoical Newfoundland is whipped by the winds from the Atlantic. It

11

draws its charm from the fishing villages huddled around the rugged coast. The province includes Labrador, snowbound for more than half the year. The Maritime Provinces—Nova Scotia, Prince Edward Island and New Brunswick—are a shade more sheltered, graced in their interior with sleepy farms, orchards and pine forests. For the world market, the Maritimes' cod is king, but for gourmets, Nova Scotia's lobster makes a more delicate kettle of fish.

Quebec's cascading, rock-strewn rivers crisscross the province from the St. Lawrence Seaway to the Hudson Bay; they provide limitless hydroelectric power for use both at home —where Canadians refer to electricity as "hydro"—and in the United States. The forests that cover the Laurentian Mountains furnish pulp, paper and construction timber, with an occasional clearing for ski resorts.

Ontario is Canada's hub. It shares four of the five Great Lakes with the U.S., but keeps for itself the best access to Niagara Falls. With transportation its major activity, the province dominates Canada's industry and commerce, even more so since financial power shifted

Reflected against Vancouver's night sky, a modern skyscraper encroaches on old Victoriana.

12

from Montreal to Toronto thirty years ago. The land is blessed with lush pastures and rich seams of nickel, uranium, iron, copper, gold and silver. Almost as an afterthought in a country where federal power is heavily diluted by the provinces, Ontario is also the home of the national capital, Ottawa.

Breadbasket not just to Canada but also to the former Soviet Union and to Asia, the wheatfields of the Prairie Provinces of Manitoba and Saskatchewan stretch to infinity, a landscape broken only by an occasional battery of giant grain elevators. The prairies continue into Alberta, but its cattle ranches and oil industry in the foothills of the Rocky Mountains set it apart as the beginning of Canada's West, home of the rodeo and Calgary Stampede.

For British Columbia, those Rockies are more of a barrier than a link to the rest of Canada. The province seems happy to nestle up against the Pacific Ocean with, at least in its southern portion, the mildest weather the country has to offer. The ocean is an abundant provider of salmon. Vineyards and orchards line the fertile valleys of the interior. But even more than in other provinces, timber is the lifeblood of B.C. The lumberjack's legendary image was created here in forests covering two-thirds of the land and boasting in the Douglas fir the most majestic of the country's evergreens.

And the Canadians themselves? Their quest for an identity continues, torn between the insistent influence of that American culture across the border and the more remote but strong emotional pull of the Old World. Canadians still celebrate Queen Victoria's birthday in May as a national holiday—providing the occasional excuse for counter-demonstrations by Quebec separatists. The town of Victoria, B.C.'s capital, is more "English" than most visiting Englishmen can bear, while neighbouring Vancouver looks more often down its coast to Seattle and San Francisco than back east to fellow Canadian cities. If Montrealers keep an eye on what's going on in Paris, the people of Toronto are less interested in London than New York, Detroit and Chicago.

National identity is further diluted by fierce regional rivalries. The newly prosperous West is eager to assert itself over the traditional power bases of Ontario and Quebec. The perennially poorer Atlantic provinces are wary of everybody, and in the Yukon and Northwest Territories, Indians and Inuit are impatient to obtain the privileges of full provincial status.

Setting aside the special situation of the native peoples (see p. 34), the rest of the population does not divide neatly into Anglo- and French-Canadians. The proud French-speaking Canadians are indeed a recognizable entity, 25 per cent of the national population concentrated mostly in Quebec but with important minorities in Ontario and New Brunswick. Their separate language and ongoing struggle for a "distinct society" has given them a much stronger sense of identity, especially apparent in contemporary literature and cinema.

But for the others, does it make sense to lump over a

Calgary cowboys will twang you a cheerful welcome to their not-too-wild West.

million of German extraction, 750,000 Italians, half a million Ukrainians and hundreds of thousands of Chinese, Indians, Pakistanis, Portuguese, Poles and Jews from Eastern Europe and North Africa under the heading "Anglos"—even if English has become their first language? Property tax forms in Toronto are printed in four different languages. While maintaining their religious and other ethnic traditions, many have their own newspapers, radio and television stations and have brought from their "old country" a more spicy alternative to the all-too-pervasive Anglo-Saxon cuisine. You'll be very grateful for Vancouver's Chinatown, Toronto's trattorias and Montreal's Jewish delicatessens. And those 40 per cent who do claim British origin are quick to let you know when they're Scots, Welsh or Irish rather than English. The Scots in particular are proud of their Macdonalds, Mackenzies and company providing the first prime ministers and dominating banking and railway management, the fur and timber trades.

In the end, Canadians are united, despite the divisive forces of regional and ethnic rivalries—and almost despite themselves —by the enduring challenge of that great, tough and still largely untamed land of theirs. Take a look.

HISTORY

Is it history or blarney to suggest that St. Brendan, a 6th-century monk from Galway, was the first European to reach Canada? The good people of Newfoundland, where he is said to have landed, like to think he was. After all, on his return, he told of being attacked by insects as big as chickens. "Of course," say the Newfies, "they must have been our giant mosquitoes!"

A more serious claim is made for the Vikings, who seem to have sailed to the coast from Greenland around the year 1000. That is the carbon dating of tools, utensils and vestiges of houses, workshops and even an iron foundry dug up at L'Anse aux Meadows on the northern tip of Newfoundland.

Which takes some of the wind out of the sails of John Cabot, the Venetian navigator who claimed Canada's eastern seaboard for England's Henry VII in 1497. Locals fight over whether it was Nova Scotia or Newfoundland he actually discovered. Cabot himself mistook it for the north-east coast of Asia. In fact, Breton, Basque and Portuguese fishermen had been there long before him but kept to themselves the secret of the coastal waters' teeming cod fisheries. Initially, the English were attracted to Canada only by the fish, preferring to concentrate their colonizing activities further down the American coast.

The French came looking for gold and diamonds, spices and a passage to Asia. In 1535 Jacques Cartier ventured up the St. Lawrence as far as Hochelaga village, dominated by a hill he named Mont Réal (Mount Royal). Cartier was not exactly showered with honours when he returned with eleven barrels of worthless yellow iron pyrites and glittering quartz. For the next 70 years, Canada was all but ignored until the French turned to the more lucrative new fur trade.

The strange European comings and goings were observed by native peoples whose ancestors had preceded these "discoverers" by at least 12,000, some of them 55,000, years. Waves of Siberian hunters had crossed a land bridge over the Bering Straits in pursuit of mammoth and bison. They spread through Alaska, south along the Pacific coast to the region of British Columbia and later east across the Yukon and Northwest Territories.

New France

With no written culture to document it, the pre-European history of the Inuit and Indians is a vague archaeological patchwork of bones, stones and artefacts. Their brief encounters with Atlantic fishermen left little impact, but the advent of French and later British colonizers brought, in exchange for their beaver pelts, all the mixed blessings of copper kettles and guns, blankets and brandy, Christianity, measles and smallpox.

After winters on the Bay of Fundy had proved too harsh, geographical expert Samuel de Champlain and his first batch of French settlers left Nova Scotia and moved over to the St. Lawrence River in 1608. Within ten years, both tenant farmers *(habitants)* and fur traders *(coureurs de bois*, literally wood-runners) were colonizing Quebec—New France—at the point where the river narrows.

What's in a Name?

Canada's first settlers have had a hard time persuading the rest of us to call them by names they consider respectable. Christopher Columbus's mistaken idea of where he had landed stamped one group as Indians, while most Arctic dwellers became known as Eskimos, an Abnaki-Indian nickname meaning "eaters of raw flesh". The latter have at last imposed their own language's more dignified name of Inuit ("The People"), but Indians have an uphill struggle asserting their vernacular equivalent, Dene. At least the country's name comes from the Algonquin Indians: Kannata ("settlement").

To guarantee each *habitant* equal access to the waterfront, the farmland was divided into long narrow strips reaching down to the river banks. Local conditions were exploited with traditional French ingenuity. Manure, for instance, was shipped downriver by heaping it on ice floes during the spring thaw. Tough *coureurs de bois* sought furs from the Huron in Ontario and Algonquin in Quebec, quickly learning language and customs and even marrying into the tribes.

Meanwhile, the huge untapped fur resources of northern Quebec and Ontario attracted the renewed attention of the British.

European buttons highlight traditional motifs on the Indians' ceremonial blankets.

In 1610, navigator Henry Hudson thought he had located the fabled Northwest Passage for his London backers when, rounding the northern tip of Quebec and heading south, he hoped, to China, he found himself locked in a vast bay on which he left his life and name. Over 50 years later, the bay was explored by two enterprising Frenchmen, Pierre Esprit Radisson and Médard Chouart des Groseilliers (known to Anglo-Canadian schoolchildren as "Radishes and Gooseberries"). Exasperated by the cost of the haul to Quebec and by the heavy taxes imposed on fur pelts, they sought a new outlet for the fur trade. Fearing a commercial threat to the St. Lawrence river, the governor in Quebec opposed their survey of the region.

This decision proved to be the beginning of the end for New France, for Radisson and Groseilliers promptly sold their idea to British merchants, who in 1670 founded the Hudson's Bay Company. Charles II granted this tentacular private joint-stock company control of all territories draining into Hudson Bay; they were named Rupert's Land after the king's cousin, who was also titular head of the company. Its initials H.B.C. came to mean "Here before Christ". And here to stay.

The first British fur traders were much less adventurous than the French, waiting for the Indians to bring their pelts to the trading post rather than seeking them out in the forest. The *coureurs de bois* were more adapted to the wilderness and understood the Indians better. From them they learned to make swift, light birchbark canoes, snowshoes, and pemmican—a ghastly but nourishing mixture of buffalo fat with bits of dried meat and berries. The French also offered higher quality goods. The H.B.C. was a penny-pincher, and Indians soon spotted—and spat out—its raw London gin tinctured with iodine to imitate French brandy.

But Britain backed this vested interest with tough diplomacy and a powerful navy, while Louis XIV was too wrapped up in his European power plays to pay much attention to French Canada. Although the British made no military conquests there during the War of Spanish Succession (1700–13), their negotiators forced the French in the ensuing Treaty of Utrecht to give up all of Acadia (Nova Scotia) except Cape Breton. There, the French fortress of Louisbourg, which defended the sea approaches to Quebec, was seized by the British in 1744. It was returned four years later in diplomatic negotiations, only to fall once and for all in 1758 in an assault mounted

19

from the new British naval base of Halifax. In the final struggle for Quebec, the courageous French military commander, Marquis de Montcalm, led outnumbered troops to a fine victory at Ticonderoga. But, poorly coordinated with local Canadian militia, they lost the city of Quebec in 1759 to Britain's General James Wolfe on the Plains of Abraham. Both Montcalm and Wolfe were killed in the battle.

The French army burned its flags and sailed home, followed by most of the merchants and colonial leaders, leaving the *habitants* to fend for themselves. After 150 years of courageous struggle against the harsh Canadian wilderness, New France was abandoned, the old country displaying a cruel lack of enthusiasm for what Voltaire dismissed as *quelques arpens de neige*—"a few acres of snow".

The British Take Over

At first, British immigrants did not exactly flock to Canada either. Governor James Murray sympathized with the Québécois, whose bravery he much admired. Although the established church was now Anglican, Catholic privileges and tithes were restored. These were enshrined in the Quebec Act of 1774, which also maintained French civil law alongside British criminal law and gave French Catholics seats on an appointed governmental council. But when American revolutionaries invaded Quebec in 1775 in the hope of winning the French-Canadians over to their cause, the latter did not rally to the British side until the American soldiers started taking the *habitants'* livestock and supplies.

When American Independence was declared, some 40,000 Loyalists—New Englanders and Ger-

20

mans from Pennsylvania, but also Indians and black African slaves—moved north to Canada. The most resilient settled on Prince Edward Island and in Nova Scotia, around the Bay of Fundy, while a majority migrated to Niagara and the Eastern Townships in southern Quebec.

To cope with the rival claims of Loyalists and Québécois, the Constitutional Act of 1791

The prairies were opened up by tough old buzzards who'd been to hell and back—and the dogs went, too.

divided the colony into Upper Canada (Ontario) and Lower Canada (Quebec), separated by the Ottawa River. Under lieutenant governors, each province had a parliamentary system modelled on the Houses of Commons and Lords, while Lower Canada's French language, civil and

21

religious institutions were safeguarded.

The land west of Ontario was written off as one big empty wilderness until Alexander Mackenzie completed the first transcontinental crossing, and Simon Fraser and David Thompson mapped out the rivers and mountains of British Columbia and the Rockies. The Hudson's Bay Company fought for control of the fur trade with the North West Company, formed in 1783. The Nor'westers commandeered the French system of forts, depots and canoe brigades; they intermarried with Indians and produced new clans of Métis. After years of fierce armed struggle for trading posts around Hudson Bay and Lakes Winnipeg and Superior, the Nor'westers threw in their lot with the H.B.C., bringing a wilder, more imaginative spirit to the staid old company.

With great pioneering skill, Upper Canada's first lieutenant governor, John Simcoe, pushed new highways north from Lake Ontario and west to Hamilton. He established the provincial capital at a trading post, Toronto, in the heart of a malarial swamp, and renamed it York. A landed gentry made up of army officers, government officials and commercial speculators ran the province, creating a hereditary aristocracy known as the Family Compact. More Americans were lured over the border with land grants; in 20 years the population rose from 14,000 to 90,000 by 1812. French-Canadians were also multiplying rapidly, from 60,000 when New France was abandoned in 1760 to 330,000 fifty years later.

Canada bore the brunt of U.S. hostility in the War of 1812. The Americans were convinced that the British were backing Indian raids on American settlements along the Canadian border. Congress called for nothing less than the conquest of Canada, but Major-General Isaac Brock's tiny Canadian force, allied with Chief Tecumseh's Shawnee Indians, routed a half-hearted American invasion along the Niagara frontier. The Americans burned and looted York, provoking a violent British reprisal raid on Washington.

Though greatly outnumbered, Anglo- and French-Canadians fought victoriously side by side at Châteauguay. But after the war, the militia of Louis-Joseph Papineau's *patriotes* became the backbone of growing anti-British agitation. With British immigration on the increase, Québécois autonomy was threatened by moves towards one government for Lower and Upper Canada. Land-owners such as Papineau feared being swamped by projected improvements of the St. Lawrence trade route. In the general paranoia, the *patriotes* even accused the British of fostering Quebec's 1832 cholera epidemic. Papineau asked London for guarantees of autonomy for a Lower Canada assembly dominated by French-Canadians. British rejection in 1837 led to riots opposing *patriotes* and British militia. After a victory at St-Denis, the French-Canadians were crushed by governor John Colborne's troops north of Montreal. *Habitants'* farmhouses were burned down, earning Colborne the nickname of Old Firebrand *(Vieux Brûlot)*, and defeat left an even more enduring bitterness than the original British conquest. Papineau fled to the United States.

In the same year, hatred of the high-handed Tory oligarchy in Upper Canada provoked a rebellion among small farmers and tradesmen beset by economic depression. Their champion, newspaper editor and first mayor of Toronto, William Lyon Mackenzie, proposed a U.S.-style republic. Heeding his call of "Up then, brave Canadians, get ready your rifles and make short work of it", a few hundred irregulars gathered at Montgomery's Tavern north of Toronto. But a Tory militia led by bagpipes put down the so-called Mackenzie Rebellion in a skirmish lasting just a few minutes. Short work indeed.

Governor General "Radical Jack" Durham was sent to put the house in order; he proposed a unified assembly governing Canada's domestic affairs. He scorned the Québécois for "retaining their peculiar language and manners. They are a people with no history and no literature." But Lower Canada's pragmatic Louis-Hippolyte Lafontaine accepted the British framework as a means of asserting the Québécois' right to equal representation. In the new United Provinces of Canada set up in 1841, he formed a delicate alliance with Toronto reformist Robert Baldwin.

Immigration increased to meet an ambitious public works programme of canals to bypass the St. Lawrence rapids and cross the Niagara peninsula, as well as new cities, mines and roads.

But the big news was railways. The first, in 1836, was the Champlain and St. Lawrence Railroad, a few miles of track between Montreal and Lake Champlain. By 1854, over 250 miles joined Niagara and Windsor. The dream of a transcontinental railway with prodigious freight revenues drew fast-fingered financiers to the Grand Trunk project to join up Montreal, the Great Lakes and the western hinterland. But initially they had to content themselves with luring American trade to the St. Lawrence by linking eastern Canadian cities to Portland, Maine.

Choosing a permanent capital for these United Provinces wasn't easy. In the perennial Anglo-French conflict, bilingual Montreal was too troublesome, while English-speaking Toronto or French-speaking Quebec City would favour one community at the expense of the other. Royal Engineer officers sent watercolours of likely sites for Queen Victoria's approval. The choice went to Bytown, a puny lumber depot renamed Ottawa after the river on which it stood, diplomatically situated between Upper and Lower Canada.

To the east, and remote from the centres of power, the people of Newfoundland and the Maritime Provinces lived in small, isolated communities with no unifying geography comparable to the Great Lakes or St. Lawrence River. Newfoundland turned its back on the hostile interior to reap the harvests of the sea. Always psychologically closer to London than to Ottawa, Newfoundland did not become part of Canada until 1949. Yankee Loyalists struggled valiantly with

a region they called Nova Scarcity. The British had scattered Nova Scotia's French Acadians, some to the nearby islands of St. Pierre and Miquelon (still French today), others as far as Louisiana, while a small nucleus remained in New Brunswick. The potential of Prince Edward Island's fertile soil was squandered by absentee land speculators who milked it only for the rent and

Stoical French soldiers beat the retreat at Louisbourg's fortress as the British advanced from Halifax.

24

left the settlers no motivation to develop it.

Even further away, the west was still administered as a separate empire by the H.B.C. until gold discovered in the Queen Charlotte Islands in 1852 and on the Fraser River six years later prompted Britain to set up a new colony to control the influx of unruly American fortune-hunters. The company's chief factor James Douglas became first governor of British Columbia. The company tried to keep Upper Canada farmers from migrating to the Prairies by depicting a sub-Arctic wasteland. But British surveyors found the valleys of the Saskatchewan, Assiniboine and Red rivers to be fertile and ideal for agriculture. The western trek began. The nation was taking shape.

Confederation

The British North America Act of 1867 created the Dominion of Canada. John A. Macdonald, an Ontario Tory, was the first prime minister. To resist a turbulent U.S.A. torn by civil war, Anglo-Canadians wanted a strong central government delegating little more than municipal affairs to the provinces. French-Canadians insisted on a federal system with stronger provincial governments, to protect specific Québécois interests in property and civil rights. Henceforth, national unity always played second fiddle to ethnic, religious and above all economic regional interests.

Only the promise of a transcontinental railway brought Nova Scotia immediately into the Confederation, British Columbia in 1871 and Prince Edward Island in 1873. Rupert's Land was bought from the H.B.C. in 1869, but incorporating Manitoba was not so easy. Led by Louis Riel, Métis descendants of Indians and French fur traders waged an armed struggle for land rights on the Red River in the face of the expansion-hungry railway builders. An impassioned politician as well as a fiery military leader, Riel won over local Anglo-Saxon support for his proposed Manitoba Act guaranteeing equal French and English language rights in school and church. But the execution of a troublemaker from Toronto brought in a retaliatory force of Ontario troops, and Riel fled to the United States. The Métis were driven off their fertile land and back to hunting on the plains.

The railway literally created new cities like Winnipeg and Vancouver, the western terminus. Against all the experts' advice, the Canadian Pacific Railway Company's general manager, William Cornelius Van Horne, built the tracks around Lake Superior and west across the Prairies to meet Andrew Onderdonk's Chinese labourers working their way east through Kicking Horse Pass in the Rockies. The transcontinental dream became reality when the tracks were joined in 1885. But along the way, scores of labourers had died hacking through the mountains, the prairies' buffalos were exterminated, and Indians and Métis dispossessed of their lands.

These were booming times. Less spectacular than the completion of the C.P.R. but economically vital, the first hydroelectric installation began functioning on Niagara Falls in 1895. A year later, gold was struck in the Klondike, opening up the Yukon to 100,000 panhandlers and camp-followers. The Prairie Provinces profited from soaring worldwide wheat exports.

Presiding over this new

prosperity was the country's first French-Canadian prime minister, Wilfrid Laurier, an elegant, eloquent Liberal. Perfectly bilingual, he was determined to forge Anglo- and French-Canadians into one nation, comparing them to the waters of the Ottawa river and Great Lakes meeting below the island of Montreal: "parallel, separate, distinguishable and yet one stream, flowing within the same banks." Visiting London for Queen Victoria's Diamond Jubilee, he charmed his hosts by declaring: "I am British to the core." He was knighted on the spot.

But Laurier saw the limits of British support when the British and American negotiators of the Alaska boundary tamely accepted the U.S. claims to a southern coastal "panhandle", which denied Canada sea access to the Yukon goldfields. He asserted greater national autonomy by taking over British military installations and shipyards at Esquimalt on Vancouver Island and Halifax, Nova Scotia. When Alberta and Saskatchewan acceded to provincial status in 1905, and the country's mining, lumber, paper and pulp industries burgeoned, Laurier championed a new transcontinental railway that would take a more northerly route to serve them—the state-owned Canadian National Railway (C.N.R.).

Laurier's conciliatory efforts did not diminish Anglo-French Canadian differences. Conflicts raged over the denial of equal rights to Catholic schools in Manitoba and a Prohibition referendum (blocked only by wine-drinking Québécois). The Québécois were slow to jump on the wagon of industrial progress. Political leader Henri Bourassa and influential editor Jules-Paul Tardivel insisted on time-honoured rural traditions. "Our mission is to possess the soil, not to pursue "American" obsessions with industry and money. They resented the sending of Canadian troops to South Africa to support the British in the Boer War and were no more enthusiastic about the Anglo-French alliance in World War I. Bourassa said: "The real enemies of French-Canadians are not the Germans but English-Canadian anglicizers, the Ontario intriguers or Irish priests."

The Twentieth Century
Under Tory government, the country supported Britain with 500,000 men in World War I and lost over 60,000 on the battlefield. Emotional European nationalism spread to Canada. Citizens of German and Austrian origin were dismissed from public service, the German language banned in schools and Berlin, Ontario, renamed Kitchener.

FACTS AND FIGURES

Geography: Larger in land surface than any other country, Canada covers exactly 9,970,610 sq. km. From Ellesmere Island in the Arctic south across Hudson Bay to Lake Erie's Middle Island, a crow would have to fly 4,634 km. Its east–west trip from Cape Spear, Newfoundland, to the Yukon-Alaska border covers 5,154 km. Canada shares with the U.S.A. the Great Lakes of Ontario, Erie, Huron and Superior. Countless rivers include the Mackenzie and Yukon in the north, the St. Lawrence flowing from Lake Ontario to the Atlantic, the Saskatchewan through the Prairie Provinces and the Columbia and Fraser over to the Pacific. Formed by the Rocky Mountains and the Coast Range, the Western Cordillera boasts the country's highest peak, Mount Logan in the Yukon, 5,959 m.

Population: 29,529,800 (490,000 Indians and 27,000 Inuit); 60% English mother tongue, 25% French, plus Italian, German and Asian.

Capital: Ottawa 880,000.

Major cities: Toronto (4,298,261), Montreal (3,127,242), Vancouver (1,705,887), Edmonton (875,000), Calgary (750,000), Winnipeg (652,400), Quebec City (645,550).

Government: Canada shares in the British Commonwealth's constitutional monarchy, with the Queen appointing a purely ceremonial governor general. A prime minister and his cabinet answer to a 295-member House of Commons, elected for a maximum 4-year term. In a mainly consultative Senate, 104 members (retiring at 75) are appointed on the advice of the prime minister.

The ten provinces have considerable autonomy over education, housing and natural resources, whereas the Yukon and Northwest Territories depend more directly on Ottawa.

Religion: Catholic 47.5%, Protestant 41%, Eastern Orthodox 1.5%, Jewish 1%.

But the war was good for the economy—arms manufacture, the railways and especially agriculture's huge wheat exports. Trade union membership expanded from 166,000 in 1914 to 378,000 in 1919, emphatically more radical in the west, where workers chose to assert their new organizational strength by calling for a proletarian revolution. In Vancouver and Calgary, they cheered the Bolshevik victory in Russia. The government blamed the 1919 general strike in Winnipeg on "enemy aliens", but the leaders were in fact British immigrants. In classic Canadian style, the campaign for a united national union movement fell victim to narrow regional interests: those of Ontario's tiny Communist Party and the Catholic union in Quebec.

William Lyon Mackenzie King became leader of the Liberal Party after Laurier's death. He made Canada progressively more independent of Britain. At the Imperial Conference of 1926, he won the acknowledgement that Canada was autonomous in external affairs and thus not subject to a common, British-dominated policy for the whole Empire. This led to the 1931 Statute of Westminster which effected the equality of Britain and the Dominions, thus consecrating Canada's full autonomy in home and foreign affairs. The governor general in Ottawa became the symbolic representative of the Crown rather than of the British government. But the provinces insisted the Constitution remain in London rather than let Ottawa infringe on their prerogatives.

At the same time, the country came more and more into the American economic and cultural orbit. The boom years of the 1920s saw the growth of a "branch-plant economy" with American automobile, rubber, chemical and clothing factories springing up around the Great Lakes at Hamilton, Oshawa, Windsor and Montreal. American popular culture inundated the country with the growth of radio, movies and mass-market magazines. Quebec, in particular, tried to resist the invasion, even going so far as to ban adolescents from cinemas. Apart from a spirited band of Ontario painters known as the Group of Seven seeking a distinctive "national" style, most of Canada's own artists—actors, musicians and writers—felt obliged to seek fame and fortune in New York, London or Paris.

Canada's Great Depression was felt first by farmers in the Prairie Provinces, unable to get rid of their surplus from 1928's wheat glut. Even the drought of 1929 could not ease matters, and ten more years of bad harvests meant they could not recoup their losses. Other sectors of the economy—timber, fisheries, mining and construction—ground to a halt as excessive production outstripped demand. Spirits were raised by the escapist fare of the new Canadian Radio Broadcasting Commission, today's C.B.C.—Hollywood extravaganzas and home-grown media stunts, not the least of which was the enduring hullabaloo surrounding the Dionne quintuplets, born in Ontario in 1934.

Trans-Canada Airlines, the forerunner of Air Canada, started up in 1937, and air travel soon became vital for covering the vast distances, fighting forest fires, and carrying provisions

---

Crisis Stopgap

Canada's Prairie Provinces called the Depression years the Dirty Thirties. Gales whipped away the dried-out top soil. Plagues of grasshoppers, hail and brutal unseasonal frosts did the rest, forcing the gradual conversion of farmland to cattle-pasture. For Saskatchewan, where nine out of ten families were on welfare, whole trains were commandeered to freight in food and clothing from other provinces. The prairie farmers couldn't fathom how to cook the salt cod sent from Newfoundland, so they used it instead to plug holes in the farmhouse roof.

---

and wages to remote corners of the far north. Natural enough, then, that involvement in World War II began with a British Commonwealth Air Training Plan using Canada's safer skies to prepare pilots for combat. At the outbreak of war, Canada's reputation for welcoming immigrants and refugees from all over the world was tarnished by blocking Communists and Jews from Hitler's Germany. Asked how many he would allow in, Justice Minister Ernest Lapointe said: "*None* is too many." After 1941, citizens of Japanese origin were interned and had their property confiscated.

In 1940, Mackenzie King and Roosevelt signed a joint American-Canadian defence pact and a year later integrated their countries' economies for the duration of the war. War was again good for business. Out of a population of 11,500,000, more than a million were directly working in war-allied industries, most of them in brand-new factories. Over 730,000 men and women served in the armed forces, suffering 43,000 losses. In 1942, without adequate Allied naval and air support, the high-risk amphibious raid of 5,000 Canadian troops on Dieppe proved disastrous (almost 1,000 killed, 2,000 captured). With more careful Allied planning a year later, Canadians played a distinguished role in the Sicily landings and Italy campaign, as well as the D-Day invasion of Normandy in 1944.

Social policies made important advances during and immediately after the war. In 1944, Saskatchewan elected the first socialist government in North America—the Cooperative Commonwealth Federation (C.C.F.). The Liberal government responded by appropriating much of the C.C.F.'s reform programme. But Indians and Inuit did not win the right to vote in federal elections until 1960.

Economically, the country was closer than ever to the U.S. A consumer boom accentuated branch-plant dependency on America's Canada-based manufacturers of cars, radios, TVs and refrigerators. The U.S. was also Canada's main customer for raw materials and energy in what was a veritable explosion of industrial achievement. North Manitoba nickel and Labrador iron were replacing depleted resources south of the border; huge oil strikes were made near Edmonton, Alberta, in 1947; a uranium reactor started up in Ontario in 1952; and hydroelectric plants mushroomed all across the country. The St. Lawrence Seaway was opened in 1959. Six years later, drivers could cross the entire continent on the Trans-Canada Highway.

The national culture fared less well. A Royal Commission on the Arts and Letters was spurned by prime minister Louis St. Laurent as a futile body for "subsidizing ballet dancers". While there was more cultural aid promised than ever delivered, one positive result was the foundation of the highly creative National Film Board.

Balancing domestic interests and relations with the American neighbour became increasingly delicate. The first prime minister from one of the Prairie Provinces, Saskatchewan Tory John Diefenbaker, made himself popular with the farmers by negotiating a sale of wheat surpluses to China that tripled their incomes—but unpopular with his American neighbour for doing business with the "Communist devil". In the wake of the 1962 Cuban missile crisis with the Soviet Union, the U.S. wanted Diefenbaker to accept nuclear warheads on Canadian soil. President John Kennedy attacked Diefenbaker's hesitation and prevarication, and the prime minister was defeated at the next elections after the Canadian Liberals had jumped on the American bandwagon.

Canada celebrated its centenary in 1967 with a world fair, the Montreal Expo. It was an opportunity to assert a more creative side of Quebec's identity

amid the province's growing militancy. Parallel to the world-wide independence movements in the 1960s, Québécois separatists fought elections demanding to be *"maîtres chez nous"* ("masters in our own home"). Activists let off a bomb or two to celebrate the national holiday for Queen Victoria's birthday, robbed banks and stole guns and ammunition. In 1967, De Gaulle declaimed his famous *"Vive le Québec libre!"* ("Long live free Quebec!") from Montreal City Hall, forgetting for a moment that French-Canadian leaders had sided with his Vichy enemies during World War II.

As a progressive minister of justice, reforming laws against homosexuality, divorce, birth control and abortion, Pierre Elliott Trudeau was sympathetic to the French-Canadians' demand to have their language placed on an equal national footing with English. But this sophisticated, bilingual Montreal lawyer opposed what he regarded as Quebec's tribalistic urge to exclude all things English from its own province. Elegant, witty and cosmopolitan, Trudeau became Liberal prime minister in 1968—and like Wilfrid Laurier before him, just the kind of

On the threshold of a new millennium, the sky's the limit.

French-Canadian that Anglo-Canadians love.

The Québécois were less enthusiastic. With the introduction of the birth-control pill, the province's birth-rate dropped from the highest to lowest in the nation, causing conservatives to worry at the waning influence of the Catholic Church and the prospect that French-Canadians would drown in a sea of Anglos. When René Lévesque's separatist Parti Québécois was defeated in the 1970 provincial elections by Robert Bourassa's Liberals, embittered militants of the Front de Libération du Québec (FLQ) turned to terrorism. In quick succession, they kidnapped British Trade Commissioner James Cross and murdered Bourassa's minister of labour Pierre Laporte. The country approved Trudeau's tough reaction; invoking the War Measures Act, he sent in 10,000 troops and arrested 468 militants. The FLQ was outlawed. Despite Lévesque's victory in 1976, Quebec gradually moved away from outright separatism to a militant but more limited programme, which preserved the province's specific culture by imposing the French language in schools, industry and government. Radicals were delighted by the subsequent westward exodus of Quebec's Anglo-Canadians, but in the process, Toronto was to bypass Montreal

33

in population, financial and even cultural activity.

After a brief respite in private life, Trudeau returned for what he felt was his crowning achievement, the Constitution Act of 1982, the consummation of Canada's political identity. The act transferred Canada's constitution to Ottawa by removing the old obligation to refer amendments to London, and incorporated a new Charter of Rights and Freedoms similar to the French Declaration of the Rights of Man.

Despite a referendum vote by its citizens *against* separatism two years earlier, Quebec was defiantly the only province not to sign the new constitution, feeling its cultural specificity had not been guaranteed. Tory prime minister Brian Mulroney won the Québécois over in 1987 with an accord recognizing them as a "distinct society". He appeased the other provinces by conceding important new powers in shared-cost programmes, immigration and appointments to the Supreme Court and Senate. The Indians and Inuit had also negotiated concessions for their lands and resources, but their Yukon and Northwest Territories are still a long way from full provincial status.

Canada's national unity remains a dynamic "work in progress".

NATIVE PEOPLES

Even though they now number less than half a million and have never been many more, the only people who have really embraced the whole of Canada's vast territory are the Inuit and the Indians. Apart from a few explorers, trappers, gold-diggers and oil drillers, Euro-Canadians have preferred to hug the narrow strip along the American border and know little or nothing of the northern wilderness. Canada's distinctness is more fully appreciated by a closer look at some of its "native peoples".

The Pioneers

In the beginning, as far as humans were concerned, Canada was a void. Siberian hunters crossed the ice of the Bering Straits in several waves. While the earliest, around 70,000 B.C., moved down the Pacific coast to South America, the settlement of Canada began some 15,000 years after, spreading across the continent from the Yukon and, much later, from British Columbia. By 8000 B.C., Indians were hunting caribou in Nova Scotia. Archaeologists have concluded that the

Unlike most Indians who migrated south, the Inuit stayed put in what are now the Northwest Territories.

pattern of life in the Stone Age was not so very different from what the first Europeans encountered.

In the Arctic, the stabilization of the sea level and a dramatic cooling of the climate around 1500 B.C. caused the hunters to switch from land mammals to fish, seal, walrus, whale and ice-dwelling polar bear. At the same time, these ancestors of the Inuit moved out of their skin-tents into warmer igloos of hardened snow blocks. They glided over the ice on skates of ivory or antler horn. From the Yukon, further migrations took them north to the High Arctic, south around Hudson Bay to Manitoba, east to Greenland and down the Labrador coast to Newfoundland.

For the west coast Indians, as the song says, the living was easy. The fish were indeed jumping; bountiful salmon were barbecued in the summertime, smoked for the winter. Prehistoric techniques for fishing and trapping continued right into modern times, though bone was replaced by steel for the weapons. One of British Columbia's favourite freshwater fishing sites, at Hell's Gate in Fraser Canyon, has been going strong for 9,000 years. Prairie Indians hunted buffalo by forcing the herds onto marshland, snowbanks, thin ice or over cliffs—one of these nasty surprises being known to this day

as the Head-Smashed-In buffalo jump, near Fort MacLeod, Alberta. Already in 3000 B.C. they were drying and smoking strips of meat—modern beef jerky. In Ontario and Quebec, where encroaching forests gradually dispersed the herds of caribou, the Iroquois ousted the Algonquin and settled down to cultivate maize, beans and squash, living in rectangular, multi-family longhouses.

The Inuit

The toughest of all Canadians have withstood the hardships of the far north, its icy deserts and Arctic blizzards, but were nearly wiped out by European diseases —measles, mumps and smallpox. Estimated at 81,000 in the 18th century, they now number some 21,000, living mostly in the eastern half of the Northwest Territories. In 1999, this area will be officially renamed *Nunavut,* meaning 'Our Land".

Since the 1950s, the federal government has gathered most of the Inuit together in village communities, to improve their education, medical care and general welfare. But more scattered groups in the High Arctic still prefer to live in traditional igloos, better insulated than stone houses and with an infinite supply of building materials.

An entrance tunnel with a kitchen alcove on one side and

storage alcoves on the other leads to the main living area, the characteristic snow-block dome measuring 13 to 15 feet in diameter at the base. Light is provided by whale-blubber oil lamps when there is no sun to shine through the translucent snow walls or a clear ice skylight. The igloos are often connected by a whole network of tunnels. This proved particularly convenient for the Caribou Inuit practice of co-marriage: two couples would exchange sexual partners, not in the casual wife-swapping of modern suburbia, but as a real alternate marriage, strengthening ties between two interlocking families.

Social solidarity in the Arctic cold is of course important. In one group on Hudson Bay, males became *mumiqatigiik* or dancing partners, a hilarious friendship solemnized in a ritual in which two buddies hit each other very hard on the face and shoulders, exchanged gifts and danced together until exhausted. And why do Inuit kiss by rubbing noses rather than with their lips? That way they won't stick to one another in below-freezing temperatures.

The Kwakiutl

For the relative opulence of their way of life, the Kwakiutl of British Columbia's Pacific coast on and around Vancouver Island count among the aristocrats of Canadian Indians. They harvested an abundance of fish from the ocean and rivers, not just salmon but halibut, herring, mussels and clams. From the forests, they hewed red cedar planks for handsomely crafted houses and 65-ft canoes to negotiate the coastal waters. Before European textiles arrived on the scene, they pounded cedar bark until it was supple and soft enough for weaving into capes, skirts and blankets.

The mild climate and generally easy living gave them the leisure to develop artistic talents less apparent among Indians and Inuit facing harsher conditions. Elaborate decoration went into fashioning the simplest everyday objects—clothing, baskets, storage boxes, even fish hooks. Carpentry is the proudest of Kwakiutl skills, spectacularly displayed in their totem poles. But this is not an ancient art form. The huge free-standing red cedar poles erected in front of the Indians' houses are essentially a 19th-century phenomenon, dependent for their intricate design on the chisels, steel axes, curved knives and other metal tools bartered from Europeans for the skins of sea otters. Size was originally limited to that of the poles and beams used to build the house, to which the carvings were directly attached. Then, as personal wealth diminished with

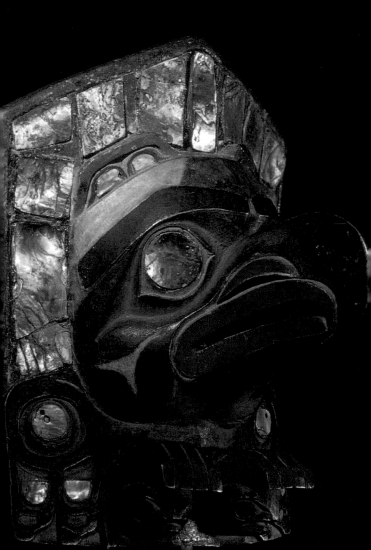

a slump in the fur trade, totem poles became prime symbols of a chief's prestige, soaring to 80 ft and more. If they survive now only in museums, especially in Vancouver (see p. 151), the ritual gift-giving known as potlatch has re-emerged after years of official prohibition. Derived from the Nootka Indian word *patschatl* meaning "to give", the potlatch traditionally enabled a chief to demonstrate his prestige to neighbouring tribes. For a year or more, he gathered up his tribe's surplus wealth—considerable during the boom years of the fur trade—to throw a huge party. In addition to a splendid feast, the host would hand out gifts of oil, carvings, jewels, prized iron tools and, above all, the coveted Hudson's Bay Company blanket, sometimes as many as 10,000 of them. While the host tribe's houses were emptied of everything except bare essentials, the guests would depart knowing that in a year or two they would have to reciprocate if they were not to lose face.

In the 1880s, the government banned this apparently wanton impoverishment, but the Kwa-kiutl, for whom wealth was measured by what they could give away, not what they kept, continued the practice clandestinely, disguising it as the distribution of Christmas presents. Today, potlatch is back in the open, updated with transistor radios and other household appliances. The blankets are now electric.

The Dene Nation

Nowhere is the clash of traditional values and modern industry more acute than in the western Subarctic. There, some 17,000 Indians from 5 tribes in the Northwest Territories sharing the Athapaskan language have joined as the Dene Nation. Together with the Métis Association (descendants of French fur traders and Plains Indians), they are involved in a perpetual tussle with private oil and natural gas companies to protect land rights and traditional culture.

Proponents of an Arctic gas pipeline passing through Indian lands in the Mackenzie Valley to northern Alberta argued that the Dene need revenues from the pipeline to escape poverty, and that in any case they no longer have an autonomous culture. They drive cars and snowmobiles, wear Western clothes, speak English, and play country-and-western music. But Dene leaders, fearful of the project's

Pacific Coast Indians decorate their house fronts with the totemic signs of their ancestors.

39

environmental impact, insisted their bush-related culture of hunting and fishing could and should be protected (through more self-government) before the pipeline was laid. Ottawa compromised with a shorter pipeline, for oil.

In fact, quite apart from the more tangible facets of Indian life that the Dene Nation is trying to preserve—language, customs, hunting and fishing grounds—it is the traditional values that remain vitally important. In the past, Indians moved around the Subarctic in small bands, with leaders not institutionalized in a sacred or hereditary role, but chosen very pragmatically for specific hunting skills or on-the-spot organizing abilities. A tough environment demanded tough qualities of interdependence and industriousness, sorely tried by contact with Europeans. The fur trade put an end to their semi-nomadic existence as they settled around the trading posts and became fiercely competitive with one another. A collapse of fur prices after World War II, while consumer goods soared, left them dependent on federal welfare.

But the bush-related culture, however precarious, is still there, and Dene leaders, still pragmatic, fight to protect it with a proper land settlement rather than dependence on pipeline revenues in a world where oil and gas prices are just as fragile as fur.

The Blackfoot

Our popular image of the North American Indian is conditioned by Hollywood's stereotype—feather headdress, necklace of scalps and whooping war dances around the campfire—in fact derived from the prairie tribes, or Plains Indians, as they are known to American anthropologists. Plains Indian folk customs and nature lore make up the bible of European boy scouts. The Blackfoot of Alberta are a classic example. Their name, says the myth, was bestowed on them when an ancestor, on his way to meet another tribe, walked through land burned by prairie fire and blackened his moccasins.

For these great hunters of the Rocky Mountain foothills and prairies, wild game included grizzly and black bear, antelope, deer, elk, wild sheep and goats, but the only "real meat" was buffalo. Before the early 1700s when horses appeared on the scene, guile was more important than speed, and the hunters

Tribal leaders wear full regalia for pow-wow on Walpole Island, Ontario.

stalked the buffalo herd disguised with the skins of wolves and buffalo calves. Horseback-hunting brought new skills and prestige to an élite given no other duties. The Blackfoot went to war with Shoshoni and Crow Indians to the south for their horses and were in turn attacked by the Cree from the north for their territory's great buffalo herds. Buffalo was everything—food, clothes and tents. Twelve to fourteen buffalo skins were needed for a single tepee. So the cultural and ecological shock was all the greater when the herds were exterminated in the 1870s. Métis and Cree Indians were devastatingly efficient with their repeater rifles, and the transcontinental railway builders made a deliberate policy of clearing the tracks of migrating buffalo. By 1877, under the Canadian government's Blackfoot Treaty, the Indians gave up their hunting ground to raise cattle on reserves.

The Micmac

Like the Indians of the Pacific Coast, the Micmac found a life of relative plenty when they migrated from the Great Lakes to the great fishing waters of Nova Scotia, Prince Edward Island and New Brunswick. The Atlantic provided a gourmet diet of oysters, clams and lobster, and the rivers teemed with salmon, eel, smelt and sturgeon. They roasted their fish whole, boiled it by dropping hot stones into the water, or ate it smoked.

Like their Algonquin cousins back in the woodlands of Quebec and Ontario, they showed a great talent for hunting—moose, beaver, bear, caribou and seal—with bow and arrow, traps and harpoon. Before the hunt, the Micmac staged a huge "eat-all" feast to clear out all available provisions, confident the larder would be amply replenished. When they returned, the hunting dogs ended up as a prize delicacy for guests at their ceremonial feasts. They lured the moose with a birchbark "horn" to imitate the female, and if that didn't work, they poured water from a birchbark receptacle into the pond to reproduce the sound of the female urinating. Once the men had killed the beast, their women had to carry it home to cook. The choice morsel was the head, roasted.

In the 18th century, the Micmac were courted by the French as allies against the British, who had them massacred by their traditional enemies, the Mohawks. But the French at Louisbourg wrought just as much mayhem among the Micmac through smallpox and typhus. Some 12,000 remain, in 27 reserves in the Atlantic provinces and Quebec.

Modern Realities

Today, the colourful folklore is being revived as an assertion of the native peoples' identity. But it is in terms of hard, everyday reality that Indians and Inuit insist on the autonomy of full provincial status for the Yukon and Northwest Territories. They are continually pressing for a greater share in the profits of the oil, uranium and other energy resources found on the lands allotted them in the 19th century, before these riches were ever dreamed of.

After years of paternalistic administration of the native peoples' property, the government now gives them a free hand in running their own businesses such as hotels and shopping centres financed from oil revenues in Alberta. Indians and Inuit prefer to mount their own campaigns against the alcoholism that is the legacy of centuries of colonial abuse, as an alternative to reliance on government-run counselling services for alcoholics. The Inuit want their own TV system and demand that local airline schedules use Inuit town names.

Beyond the issues of personal and collective dignity, the native peoples of Canada remind us that, long before Cabot and Cartier, C.P.R. and C.N.R., Diefenbaker and Trudeau, this land was theirs.

WHERE TO GO

With a country this big, how do you get to know the place as a whole? The answer is, of course, that you can't. Not even most Canadians will have seen all that you will see on a well-planned trip. A visit to Canada aiming at anything more than just one destination—Toronto, Montreal or Vancouver—is bound to seem a little intimidating. The distances to cover are so enormous. But it can be done, with the journey itself a large part of the adventure, as you zoom across the wide open spaces separating one city from another. The Berlitz-Info section at the back of this book gives detailed practical guidance, but here are some general ideas to help you plan your trip.

On a first visit, you'll probably be able to get a feel for just a few of the regions we describe, but you can capture the essence of Canada in a judicious combination of two or three major cities with the marvellous outdoor life. We do not attempt an encyclopaedic coverage of every nook and cranny from the U.S. border to the Arctic Circle, but we do provide a representative sample of the country's attractions.

Where

We've divided the country into six regions, each with at least one major town accessible by air as a "launching pad" from which to explore the hinterland: Ontario; Quebec; the Atlantic (Newfoundland and the Maritimes); British Columbia; the Rockies and the Prairie Provinces (Alberta, Saskatchewan and Manitoba); the North (Yukon and Northwest Territories).

Two suggested plans of attack are either to start in Toronto or Montreal and take in Ontario and Quebec, with side trips to the Atlantic coast or even out to the west; or to start in Vancouver or Calgary and explore the Rockies and British Columbia before heading east to Ontario or Quebec, taking in the Prairies on a cross-country train-ride. The North, on a first trip, must be considered a proposition strictly for the adventurous. In any case, count on at least three weeks, ideally a month, even to begin to do the place justice.

When

One of the great advantages of Canada's vast size is that, apart from a couple of major tourist attractions like Niagara Falls, it's never overcrowded. Even in high summer, there's still plenty of room for everybody. Nonetheless, it is advisable to make advance bookings for some resort hotels on the Pacific coast, in the Rockies or around the Great Lakes.

July and August guarantee the best weather, though it can get very hot in Montreal, Toronto and the Prairie Provinces (aggravated by the hot *chinook* wind off the Rockies). Further to the north, mosquitoes can be a problem in summer. The spectacular autumn from September to mid-October is favoured by connoisseurs of the forests of Quebec and the Maritimes. While the west coast is mild in May and June, in central and eastern Canada you'll still find snow on the ground in May and a nip in the air through the month of June. The period from November to April is strictly for winter sports enthusiasts.

Remember the old adage: there's no bad weather, only bad clothing. In addition to your light summer wear, be sure to bring a sweater for the occasional chilly evenings. Rather than weigh down your luggage with anything cumbersome, take a leaf out of the Canadians' book and keep warm with several layers. If you're thinking of going north, consider long underwear. In any case, don't forget a raincoat, especially for British Columbia where the word drought is oddly pronounced and frequently misspelled because

Take off into the wild blue yonder of the Rocky Mountains' Icefield Parkway.

there's no real reason to use it. Important everywhere is a good pair of walking shoes—something light but more solid than tennis shoes.

How

The most adventurous traveller who loves to improvise still needs a certain amount of advance planning. Canada's tourist offices are conscientious and well worth consulting, even before you leave home. The national tourist office is also helpful, but in Canada the provinces jealously protect their prerogatives against the federal government, and Quebec, Ontario, British Columbia, etc. maintain their own tourist offices and can give you detailed information about resorts, accommodation, camping and sports facilities.

To cover half a continent, air travel is invaluable. To get the cheapest deal, plan the broad outlines of your itinerary ahead of time so that you can buy your tickets before you reach Canada. The two national airlines, Air Canada and Canadian International (each linked to smaller companies flying the interior), have cut-rate multiple-flight ticketing. Helicopters and hydroplanes fly you for fishing and camping expeditions in the remoter areas. Take advantage of the boat cruises wherever you can—around Newfoundland, Halifax harbour, the Great Lakes or the Inside Passage off the Pacific coast.

For a closer look at the wide open spaces, take a train. VIA Rail is the national passenger train system using the tracks of Canadian Pacific and Canadian National, who devote themselves strictly to more lucrative freight-carrying. Serving pretty good food in comfortable diners, with club cars, observation decks and sleeping cars, VIA takes a leisurely three days from Montreal to Vancouver. (From Montreal to Toronto, it's faster by train, 4 hours, than by road.)

Buses are a possibility for the occasional excursion, but a car remains essential for independent mobility. The airlines will arrange for car rentals at each airport. The Trans-Canada Highway stretches nearly 8,000 kilometres from coast to coast, and secondary roads are very good until you get into the backwoods. Inside the major cities, you may prefer to park your car and use the generally efficient public transport. One of the best ways to explore the hinterland, especially in the national and provincial parks, is to rent a comfortably equipped mobile home or camping car. This, too, should be done in advance.

Whatever you do, Canada is not a place just to sit around in and do nothing. Get going.

ONTARIO

This choice piece of real estate between the Great Lakes and Hudson Bay is the country's dominant province—too dominant for the liking of many of the others. With over 11 million people clustered almost entirely along the southern border, Ontario is the most populous province and the wealthiest, generating close to 40 per cent of the gross national product from manufacturing, construction, minerals, forestry and agriculture. The province has grown in vitality with the influx of Italian, German, Portuguese, Caribbean, Indian and Pakistani immigrants, reducing the once overwhelming "British" majority to barely 50 per cent. If Ontarians are known for their bumptious spirit, they certainly have something to be bumptious about in their province's burgeoning towns and the riches of its farmlands, forests and lakes.

Not content with taking over from Montreal as the nation's business capital, Toronto is surging forward with a vigorous cultural and social life. Bemused visitors from across the border note how it has been possible to create a vibrant modern metropolis without the hassles of inner-city blight and violence. As the national capital, Ottawa is the inevitable butt of jokes against its federal government bureaucracy, but patriots revere its parliament and museums preserving Canada's cultural treasures.

In Niagara Falls, Ontario has, to the chagrin of many American tour operators, the best grandstand view of one of the western world's great natural wonders. Southern Ontario's countryside is a gentle green delight enhanced by theatre festivals celebrating Shaw at Niagara-on-the-Lake and Shakespeare at Stratford. Cruise around the Great Lakes, try the water sports on Georgian Bay and explore the Thousand Islands or Point Pelee nature reserve.

Ontario's history is preserved in lovingly reconstructed villages and forts marking the passage of French Jesuit missionaries at Sainte-Marie Among the Hurons, a fur-trading post at Thunder Bay, military positions at Fort George (Niagara) and Fort Henry (Kingston), and the pioneer communities at Upper Canada Village (Morrisburg) and Black Creek (Toronto).

TORONTO

Hard to believe that this gleaming citadel of big business and the good urban life was in the 1790s a malarial swamp. Muddy York once could be recommended only by its commanding position on Lake Ontario, from which Fort York guarded the troublesome American border. Today, the mud is neatly paved over, the mosquitoes have flown elsewhere, and the Americans are less trouble than they used to be. Yonge Street, the military highway which founder John Simcoe thrust north from the fort to Lake Simcoe, starts out now as downtown Toronto's main commercial artery. Its intersection at the elegant shopping thoroughfare, Bloor Street, is the fashionable hub of the city.

Getting around the city is quite simple, but while downtown park your car and walk or use the buses or subway.

Following John Simcoe's military grid pattern, Toronto's main arteries run from the lakefront north: Spadina and University avenues, Bay, Yonge

---

No Shrinking Violets

Torontonians have always had an unshakeably high opinion of their town. The founding fathers were in the main a stout bunch of upstart New Yorkers who didn't like the American Revolution. In their new home, they formed a Family Compact of financiers, bankers and lawyers and followed the fiercely stringent morals of Anglican archdeacon John Strachan to earn their city the ironic name of "Toronto the Good". For generations, they imposed strict drinking laws, solemn observance of the Sunday sabbath, "proper" dress and behaviour in public.

The Family Compact is today only a dim memory among the last scions of the FOOFs (Fine Old Ontario Families). Italians and Jews, Chinese, Greeks and Indians have brought a new colour and spice to the town. Self-confidence has zoomed after Quebec's separatist troubles drove Montreal's top Anglo-Canadian businesses into the welcoming arms of Toronto's Bay Street financiers. All five major Canadian banks have their head offices in Toronto, including the Bank of Montreal, whose president and CEO are based here. Although yuppies may have been a short-lived phenomenon of the 80s, they left one positive mark on Toronto: a demand for high-quality goods, good cuisine, bright and healthy living and an endless desire to improve the city's environment. Now they call it Toronto the Terrific. Modest, they'll never be.

and Church streets; and east–west: Front, King, Queen, Dundas, College-Carlton and Bloor streets. Our sightseeing itinerary starts down at the waterfront and works north through the business district to the chic shopping and museums area. As an alternative, especially if you have children, you may prefer to start downtown, around Union Station, and visit the other sights to the north before coming back to relax among the recreational attractions of the waterfront.

Waterfront Area

You might face severe punishment from those very proud Torontonians if you don't begin your waterfront tour with a trip up the **CN Tower**. This handsome, outsize TV antenna makes up for its unimaginative name (from its builder, the Canadian National railway and telecommunications company) with all the fanciful interpretations of its shape: jousting lance, hypodermic needle, serpent frozen rigid while swallowing a football. At 1,815 ft, it is currently the world's highest free-standing structure, 56 ft more than a similar monster in Moscow (the highest "real edifice" remains Chicago's Sears Building).

A plexiglass elevator whizzes you up the *outside* of the tower to two observation decks in the **Sky Pod**. The ride is free for those dining at the restaurant, but visitors to the nightclub must buy an observation ticket costing $12. (Incidentally, the restaurant and nightclub rank as the world's highest, if you don't count a couple in the Rockies, Alps and Himalayas. ...) The view at the top reveals a whole history of Toronto in the contrast between the glass and steel skyscraper canyons of the financial district, the geometric dome and cantilevered structures of the Ontario Place leisure complex, and the old-fashioned gabled houses of the neighbourhoods.

Take a second elevator to the **Space Deck**, to get the full sweep of Lake Ontario's so-called "Golden Horseshoe". Including Toronto, this dense urban belt from Oshawa in the east to Hamilton and St. Catharines in the west houses half the total population of the province. More romantically, you can catch a glimpse of Niagara Falls and see across the border to Buffalo.

After years of neglect, when it served only the lake's loading docks, railway depots and factories, the waterfront has become a major attraction for Torontonians at play.

Harbourfront is a bright new neighbourhood reclaimed from a swampy wasteland, at the foot of the CN Tower. Rundown warehouses and factories have been transformed into art galleries,

49

bars, restaurants, boutiques, a sailing school, playgrounds in the park and, more recently, chic apartments. Young upwardly mobile pedlars of old and new-old china and other bric-a-brac on Queen's Quay West call their

Everything is man-made at Ontario Place, even the islands.

flea market the Harbourfront Antique Market.

For a thorough view of the port facilities, take the **harbour boat tour** organized by the Toronto Harbour Commission.

Facing Harbourfront, the breezy beaches and picnic areas of the **Toronto Islands**, free of traffic, offer another handy escape from the city bustle. They were part of the Scarborough

Bluffs peninsula until storms and floods in the mid-19th century broke them up into islands, joined today by bridges. In the summer months, ferry boats leave from the docks behind the Westin Harbour Castle Hotel at the foot of Yonge Street, calling at the three main islands. No cars are allowed, but walking is, or you can rent a bicycle, downtown or on **Centre Island**. The latter is the most popular with Torontonians, and its beaches are particularly crowded at weekends. In July, it is the major focus of the great West Indian Festival of Caribana celebrating those other islands' extravagant costumes and music of steel band, calypso and reggae. At the eastern end, quieter **Ward's Island** is residential; you can join the locals for their daily constitutional on the boardwalk. To the west, swimmers favour the beach at **Hanlan's Point**, behind the Toronto Island Airport.

Jutting out from the grounds of the annual Canadian National Exhibition ("Ex" to locals), the ultramodern recreation complex of **Ontario Place** is built on three man-made islands. It combines the atmosphere of theme park and culture centre.

The outstanding landmark is the white geodesic dome of the **Cinesphere**. On a six-storey-high circular screen, it shows superb documentary films of spectacular natural phenomena such as volcanic eruptions or the latest advances in earth and space exploration. Pedalos are a delightfully lazy way of getting a duck's eye view of the attractions. Energetic 4-to-14-year-olds love the **Children's Village**, complete with trampoline and waterslide. Toddlers splash around in the duck ponds. Before you move on, put your drenched kids through the

51

huge "dryer" shaped like a bird. The older crowd heads for the outdoor **Molson** amphitheatre, seating 16,000 spectators for its classical, jazz and rock concerts. Best way to ensure good seats for the top attractions is to picnic on the grass before the show begins.

Moored at the entrance to the park is the Canadian warship **HMCS Haida**, a destroyer active in World War II and the Korean War and named after the (peace-loving) Haida Indians of British Columbia. You'll find sea cadets on board to answer your questions.

Nearby, the **Marine Museum of Upper Canada** (Exhibition Place, just west of Princes' Gate) traces the history of shipping on the St. Lawrence River and the Great Lakes, with all the brass and wooden paraphernalia of the old vessels in addition to some beautiful scale-models.

If patriots make a reverent pilgrimage to **Canada's Sports Hall of Fame** (just off Lakeshore Boulevard West) to salute heroic athletes of the past, the separate **Hockey Hall of Fame** provides a tonic lesson for American visitors to recall among the trophies, masks, skates and hockey sticks that nearly all their ice hockey heroes are Canadian-born. With the many splits between Anglo- and French-Canadians, Protestants and Catholics, ice hockey

is the closest thing the country has to a state religion.

Of all the many historic sites carefully preserved and prettied up around the country, **Old Fort York** (corner of Bathurst St. and Strachan Ave.) has one of the most bizarre locations, sandwiched between the Gardner Expressway and the railway tracks. When Lieutenant Governor Simcoe built it in 1793, it commanded a strategic position directly on the lakeshore, facing potential attack from across the American border. In the War of 1812, retreating British forces chose to destroy it rather than let it fall into American hands. It was rebuilt in 1841 and restored in 1934 as a tourist attraction, with a diorama of the Battle of York and authentically furnished 19th-century officers' quarters, log cabins and military surgery. In summertime, you can watch troops parading in the British army's famous scarlet uniforms, performing bayonet drills and firing their muskets.

Heart of Downtown

The essence of Toronto, old and new, is concentrated around **Union Station**. It was inaugurated by the Prince of Wales in 1927, when stations were still built like Greek temples—Corinthian pillars, heroic statues and ceramic-tiled ceilings—one last proud fanfare for the transcontinental railways that founded the country's industrial prosperity. In this headquarters city of Canadian National Railways, it also symbolized Toronto's position as a major commercial and industrial centre. Across the street, the venerable **Royal York** hotel, refurbished to something of its old grandeur, provides a businessmen's palace as appropriate counterpart. It is linked to the station by a large underground concourse of shops and banks.

If the station and its hotel showed where Toronto was heading, the **Metro Toronto Convention Centre** to the west proclaims the city's triumphant arrival. Currently undergoing major expansion, the present complex provides audiovisual and communications services, three main halls seating up to 12,000, banquet halls, a Grand Ball Room and sports facilities to stretch those tired executive muscles.

Providing a cultural counterpoint a block north of the Convention Centre, Vancouver architect Arthur Erickson's transparent **Roy Thomson Hall** glows at night to show off the throngs of smart concert-goers for the Toronto Symphony Orchestra. More middlebrow entertainment of bouncy Broadway musicals is to be had at the nearby Edwardian **Royal Alexandra Theatre**. This, along with the popular old-fashioned restaurants next door, was restored by discount retailing tycoon Ed Mirvish, who later endeared himself to the British theatre public by renovating London's Old Vic.

"Inland" from Union Station, the Bay Street **financial district** accentuates the town's evolution. Almost all the neoclassical limestone and marble monuments enshrining the old banks and stock exchange have been replaced by glittering steel and glass towers and tiered pyramids. **Royal Bank Plaza**, at the corner of Front and Bay streets, reflects the new prosperity in the gilded glass of its windows (treated with some 2,500 ounces of real gold). The vast lobby and atrium of the interior are correspondingly opulent, a dazzling play of cascade, ponds and greenery beneath a décor of thousands of aluminium cylinders, the work of Venezuelan sculptor Jesús Raphael Soto. If the plaza's architect Boris Zerafa is a gifted "local boy", Toronto's other banks have not hesitated to bring in talents of international renown.

In starkly austere but elegant contrast to the Royal Bank's exuberance, German Bauhaus master Mies van der Rohe designed the black steel towers for the **Toronto Dominion Centre** (between Wellington and King streets). Immediately to the east in **Commerce Court** is an exhilarating 57-storey stainless steel tower by Chinese-American architect I.M. Pei, designer of Washington's National Gallery and the Great Pyramid for the Louvre museum in Paris.

Completing the financial picture north of the Dominion Centre is **First Canadian Place**, Canada's tallest office building. In one tower is the Bank of Montreal, reached across a pleasant green courtyard with smart shops around the waterfall. The second tower houses the infinitely more boisterous new **Toronto Stock Exchange**. Behind the Exchange Tower is a trading pavilion with an observation deck for you to watch the frenetic transactions. Best hours are between 10 a.m. and 2 p.m. Mammon keeps company with the muses in the Exchange Lobby where, against a handsome setting of sculptures, paintings and Art Deco design, computer monitors give the latest prices from around the world.

A bustling underground network of concourses and escalators links the major buildings of the financial district to create a whole other neighbourhood of shopping malls, cinemas and restaurants, providing warm shelter in the winter and air-conditioned relief in the humid summer.

East of Yonge Street along Front, the **O'Keefe Centre** is a less than graceful concrete bunker in which to house the National Ballet of Canada and the Canadian Opera Company. Next door, Canadian drama is given pride of place at the **St. Lawrence Centre for the Performing Arts**. A block away at Jarvis Street, the sprawling indoor-outdoor **St. Lawrence Market** is open Tuesdays to Saturdays, with the flea market setting up its stalls here on Sundays. Buskers turn it into something of a genteel English country fair at the weekend. Good place to pick up your picnic—cooked snacks as well as fruit and vegetables—for the Islands. Nearby **St. Lawrence Hall**, once host to the freaks and darlings of Victorian vaudeville, has been beautifully restored to its original pink and green to provide a second home for the National Ballet.

In a country not renowned for its ecumenical harmony, **Church Street** lines up the Anglican St. James Cathedral, the United Church's Metropolitan Church and the Roman Catholic St. Michael's Cathedral, each an architectural variation of the neo-Gothic style of the Victorian era.

Yuppies pause for yummies at T.D. Centre.

North of Queen Street, **Nathan Phillips Square**, named after a prominent Toronto mayor, is the centre of municipal government. In the summer, ethnic communities hold their festivals and parades around the great reflecting pool. In the winter, the pool becomes a skating rink and the focus for ebullient celebrations on New Year's Eve. **Old City Hall**, grand neo-Gothic stone monument with clocktower and gargoyles, has been converted into a courthouse to make way for the striking modern landmark of **New City Hall**, designed by Finnish architect Viljo Revell. Its two gently curving office blocks open like an oyster over a domed "pearl" containing the council chamber. Henry Moore's statue of *The Archer* adorns the courtyard.

No tour of Toronto's civic past and present is complete without a pilgrimage over to Bond Street, south of Dundas, to **Mackenzie House**, home of Toronto's first and most celebrated mayor. William Lyon Mackenzie, a Dundee-born Scot, lived here after his return from exile for leading a revolt in 1837 (see p. 23). In the meticulously restored interior, guides in traditional colonial dress explain the memorabilia of the fiery newspaperman, including the hand-operated flatbed printing press on which he turned out his revolutionary newspaper, *The Colonial Advocate.*

West of Mackenzie House, at the corner of Yonge and Dundas streets, is one of Toronto's shopping "musts", the **Eaton Centre**. The late 20th-century phenomenon of the giant mall becomes here a spectacular showcase of galleries under an arched glass roof, with fibreglass geese suspended in a refreshing décor of greenery and flowers. Scores of shops and cafés are gathered above and below ground, a monument of merchandising to celebrate the century-old enterprise of this leading department store chain rivalling Hudson's Bay across the country.

West of Nathan Phillips Square, beyond tree-lined lawns, is **Osgoode Hall**, a true jewel of Georgian architecture in white limestone and amber brick, seat since 1832 of the Law Society of Upper Canada. Notice the beautiful wrought-iron "cow gates" put up at the main entrance to keep the cattle out in those early rural days. This may whet your appetite to see inside a couple of other gracious relics of the Georgian era. Visit **Campbell House** on the north-west corner of Queen and University streets. Guides in Colonial Dames' costumes will show you round the home of Sir William Campbell, Chief Justice of Upper Canada in the 1820s. At Grange Park, reached through the basement of the Art Gallery of Ontario (see p. 60), **The Grange** will show you, again with the help of costumed guides, the grand life enjoyed by members of the much admired and hated Family Compact. The Boultons built this country mansion in 1817, when its grounds stretched over 3 km from Queen clear up to Bloor Street. Note the fine winding staircase, statuary and stained-glass windows. Be sure to go below stairs, too, to visit the spacious kitchens.

On McCaul Street, across from the Art Gallery, the **Village by the Grange** tries to recreate something of this olde-worlde atmosphere for its boutiques and restaurants.

Queen's Park and Yorkville

The broad tree-lined University Avenue makes an appropriately dignified and pleasant approach to the High Victorian pink sandstone **Provincial Parliament Building** and other government offices in the middle of the oval **Queen's Park**. Guided tours will show you the principal halls and chambers. From the visitors' gallery, you can watch all the excitement of provincial parliamentary debates when in session (February to June and October to December).

West of Queen's Park is the **University of Toronto**, one of the top colleges in North America, with most of its buildings in traditional Oxbridge Romanesque-and-Gothic. The medical school has maintained a high reputation since its researchers Frederick Banting and Charles Best made their discovery of insulin in 1921. The University bookshop—known locally as book *rooms*—on College Street is the best in town.

Between Avenue Road and Yonge Street north of Bloor, **Yorkville** is the town's most appealing district to stroll around in. In a transformation no less dramatic than the Harbourfront, the hippy slum of the '60s has been refurbished into a chic neighbourhood of fashionable boutiques, art galleries, sidewalk cafés, gourmet restaurants and colourfully repainted old houses. **Hazelton Lanes** is a delightful variation on the conventional shopping mall, whereby the maze of walkways and staircases around sunken courtyards is deliberately designed to get you lost until you buy or eat your way out.

You might very easily walk right past the unprepossessing façade of the **Metro Toronto Library** (on Yonge one block north of Bloor), but the subtly interconnected areas of architect Raymond Moriyama's striking

57

Kensington Market neighbourhood has been spruced up by a lick of paint.

interior may tempt you to give up your vacation and get down to some solid study. Five floors of book stacks in a décor of orange and burnt sienna surround a brilliant atrium filled with greenery, fountain and reflector pool, while a transparent elevator zips silently up and down.

Crazy **Casa Loma**, north-west of Yorkville at 1 Austin Terracc, is Toronto's answer to California's Hearst Castle. Its battlements and turrets are all a self-respecting financier like Henry Pellatt could have wished for. After touring the castles of Europe for a few ideas, he built the 98-room mansion in the early 1900s at the then astronomical cost of $3,500,000. He chose his oak and walnut from North

Room and the stained-glass dome, marble floors and Italianate bronze doors of the Conservatory. Take the long tunnel from the wine cellar to the stables, where the horses were spoiled silly with a home of Spanish tile and mahogany.

The Ethnic Neighbourhoods

In typical North American style, Toronto's ethnic communities move around as they grow more affluent or as new construction pushes them out. The high rises and parking garages behind the New City Hall forced **Chinatown** to move west. The community, more recent immigrants than the railway labourers who settled on the west coast, have set up their restaurants, exotic hardware stores and herbal medicine shops along Dundas Street and Spadina Avenue. Look in at the pagoda-roofed **China Court** shops grouped around a little Chinese garden.

Other ethnic groups—Portuguese, Greeks, Italians, West and East Indians—buy and sell at nearby **Kensington Market**, west of Spadina. It has the delightful, exotic chaos of a bustling bazaar, best of all on Saturday mornings.

The Jews who once inhabited this Kensington Market area have moved to smarter **Forest Hill**, north-west of Casa Loma.

America, teak from Asia, panelling, marble and glass from Europe. With all the terraces, massive walls and echoing rooms, it isn't exactly cosy, which may explain why Pellatt provided himself with a secret escape route through a hidden staircase leading from his study (and now open to the public). Whatever folly of grandeur the financier entertained is best seen in the opulently panelled Oak

59

You'll find the *souvlaki* restaurants and *bouzouki* music of **Little Athens** across the Don River on Danforth Avenue, home of the first Italian immigrants. **Little Italy**, actually shared with the Portuguese, is located around Dufferin and St. Clair West.

Museums

Undergoing an ambitious programme of renovation, the richly endowed **Royal Ontario Museum**, popularly known as the ROM (100 Queen's Park), has won international recognition for its collections of Chinese, Egyptian, Greek and Roman antiquities, as well as the art of North American Indians and Inuit.

The magnificent **Chinese Collection** (renamed the **T.T. Tsui Galleries of Chinese Art** as from February 1996) presents the objects and ornaments of some 3,500 years of civilization stretching from the Bronze Age Shang Dynasty to the extinction of the Manchu Dynasty in 1912, when China became a republic. As well as the new Early China Gallery, exhibits include ceramic figures of the imperial court and the Ming Tomb (or Chinese Tomb). The captions on the showcases do a fine job of placing the exhibits in a living context, explaining, for instance, the way a house was designed to deal with the changing elements and seasons, or the religious significance of the figurines that people the tomb.

The bulk of the collection was assembled by fur trader George Crofts after he settled in the port of Tianjin; it was continued after his death in 1925 by the Anglican Bishop of Hunan, William Charles White. The **Bishop White Gallery** features Buddhist and Taoist frescoes of the 13th-century Yuan Dynasty, under Emperor Kublai Khan, along with some monumental polychrome and gilt wooden statues of the Buddha.

Across the street from the ROM, the **George R. Gardiner Museum of Ceramic Art** offers a very attractive way of acquiring an instant history of ceramics from 2000 B.C. to the 18th century. The huge collection includes pre-Columbian earthenware figures, brilliant Italian Renaissance Maiolica, more sedate but elegant Dutch and English Delftware of the 16th and 17th centuries and the Rococo forms of German Meissen porcelain.

In front of the **Art Gallery of Ontario** (AGO), 317 Dundas Street West, an intense Henry Moore bronze, *Large Two Forms*, proclaims the museum's outstanding feature: North America's finest collection of the Briton's works. The **Henry Moore Sculpture Centre** occupies a whole wing designed by the artist himself. The 600 pieces of the collection shown on a rotation basis comprise major works, small-scale bronze models, sketches and paintings. But it's the great plaster casts in their sometimes brutal original state that give the visitor a unique opportunity to see a representative sample of the monumental pieces that grace public squares and university quadrangles all over the world. Besides the celebrated reclining figures, look out for the formidable skull-like design from which the *Nuclear Energy* monument was cast for the University of Chicago.

That's no halo, just static electricity at the Ontario Science Centre.

The AGO's **Walker Gallery** exhibits sculpture by fellow Briton Barbara Hepworth, as well as Rodin, Degas and Maillol. The **European collection** of paintings includes important classical works by Tintoretto, Rembrandt, Van Dyck, Rubens, Frans Hals, Jan van Goyen and Poussin. An Ontario collection inevitably gives a prominent place to British painters such as Hogarth, Raeburn, Reynolds and Gainsborough. Among the Impressionists and their followers represented here are Renoir, Pissarro, Monet, Cézanne and Van Gogh. "Moderns" include Matisse, Picasso and Braque. The **Canadian collection** provides a comprehensive survey of 200 years of Canadian painting, pride of place going to Emily Carr, Tom Thomson and members of the influential Group of Seven.

Two museums on the city outskirts are well worth the excursion. The marvellously entertaining **Ontario Science Centre** stands 10 km north-east of the city centre, at 770 Don Mills Road. This is not another dreary scientific museum where people file past glass cases of mystifying machinery and jars of assorted animal organs. Here, adults and children are expected to participate, and they do so enthusiastically in what turns into a sophisticated push-button play centre, focused as much on the future as the past and present and proving that serious science can be fun.

The Centre's design, in a lovely green ravine of the Don River Valley, makes an exciting first impression. Architect Raymond Moriyama has linked up the Centre's several buildings with escalators and passageways like a series of atomic nuclei, comparable to his work on the various spaces and levels of the Metro Toronto Library.

Inside, it's one thing to remember what your teacher told you about static electricity, it's quite another to touch (without risk) the Centre's 300,000-volt sphere and see your hair stand on end. You can man the controls of a space-vehicle for a simulated moon-landing, broadcast your voice clear around the world through a parabolic sound reflector or find out what goes on off-camera in a fully equipped TV studio.

The **McMichael Canadian Collection** (in the village of Kleinburg, 40 minutes' drive north-west of Toronto) consecrates the work of Canada's most important school of painting, the Group of Seven. For these artists of the first half of the 20th century, who sought the sources of their inspiration in a distinctly Canadian landscape rather than the derivative themes of European painting, the museum has chosen an appropriate setting of evergreen forest overlooking the Humber Valley. The stone and log building is itself, in more solid form, a visual reference to the log cabins of the country's earliest settlers. Beside the Group's striking landscapes, look out, too, for the Inuit and Indian art, most notably the work of Norval Morrisseau, a Midéwiwin Indian from northern Ontario treating traditional subjects with a modern abstract technique.

Black Creek
Pioneer Village

(Half-hour drive north-west of downtown Toronto to Jane Street and Steeles Avenue.) Conservationists have re-created on a 19th-century farm something of the original atmosphere of an early Ontario log-cabin village. In horse-drawn carts you visit costumed villagers tilling and harvesting, sheep-shearing, grinding flour in the mill, weaving, fashioning horseshoes in the smithy. Home-cooked meals are served at the posthouse inn.

The Group of Seven

Following the powerful inspiration of Tom Thomson, who died in 1917, Lawren Harris, J.E.H. MacDonald, Franklin Carmichael, Arthur Lismer, Francis Johnston, A.Y. Jackson and Frederick Varley staged their first exhibition as the Group of Seven in Toronto in 1920. Their work fits into Canada's perpetual quest for a national identity set apart from the U.S.A. and Europe. "An art," said Jackson, "must grow and flower in the land before the country will be a real home for its people."

Rejecting Europe's refinement and delicate technique, the Group painted with a deliberately raw and coarse vitality that corresponded more closely to the Canadian

experience in its tough northern climate. To explore the country's remoter regions, these mostly Ontario-born artists took off by train to the Rockies and the North, living and painting out of a railway box-car.

But they were not impervious to the prevailing winds of modern art across the Atlantic. As you'll see in the McMichael Collection, the stark colour and often jagged forms of Canada's mountains, forests and lakes progressively took on a more abstract and even Cubist treatment. And like their European counterparts, they were assaulted by the more conservative critics. When MacDonald exposed The Tangled Garden, for example, he was accused of "throwing his paint pots in the face of the public."

NIAGARA PENINSULA

The 90-minute drive from Toronto to Niagara Falls curves around the west end of Lake Ontario through the province's industrial heartland—Mississauga, Hamilton and St. Catharines—known as the Golden Horseshoe. If you want to see the Falls without getting entangled overnight in the mob scene of the tourists (12–15 million visitors annually), stay over in the quieter town of Niagara-on-the-Lake, a bare half hour's drive away.

Niagara Falls

The true marvel of Niagara is how nature still manages to triumph over tawdry commercialism, perhaps less strident on the Canadian than on the American side of the border marked by the Falls. No amount of pushy pedlars or tacky pink honeymoon motels (if you do stay overnight, ask to see one of the hilarious bridal suites) can diminish the spectacle of that mass of white water taking its awesome plunge on the way from Lake Erie towards Lake Ontario.

Mere statistics—an average of 100,000 cubic feet of water per second generating 4 million kilowatts of energy—convey nothing of the falls' enormity, but a

Niagara attracts a bizarre monastic order in yellow rubber raincoats.

close-up view is unforgettable. The Niagara River divides in fact into two major cascades around Goat Island: to the east, **American Falls** (70-110 ft high with a crestline of 1,076 ft) and to the west, the more dramatic Canadian **Horseshoe Falls** (170 ft high with a curving crestline of 2,214 ft), and a smaller cascade off to the side, known as Bridal Veil.

There are several vantage-points from which to view the Falls. **Table Rock**, named after a ledge that's long since fallen in the river, is right on the brink of Horseshoe Falls. Down below, the Table Rock Scenic Tunnels take you *behind* the mighty wall of water. With the price of the ticket, you borrow some protective clothing, but nothing is totally waterproof against Niagara. Don't let that worry you—seeing Niagara and not getting wet would be silly. Just keep a dry change of clothing in the car. A boat tour in one of the three vessels that go by the name of *Maid of the Mist* takes you past and damply close to both American and Horseshoe Falls. The *Spanish Aero* cable car gives you a bird's-eye view of the Niagara Whirlpool rapids. For an overall view, try the Skylon and Minolta towers or the more expensive but spectacular helicopter service (at Victoria Avenue and Niagara Parkway) which flies over the

Barrelling Over

In 1859, the French tightrope walker Blondin made his way across Niagara Falls on a high wire. Subsequently, others came into closer contact with the waters by going over the Horseshoe Falls in a barrel or reinforced rubber ball. (Some of the contraptions used for these crazy leaps are on show at the Niagara Falls Museum, 5651 River Road.) Ten have made the plunge, but only seven survived to tell the tale. The first to go over, in 1901, was a woman, Annie Taylor, hoping to make money from the publicity. She went on tour as "Queen of the Mist", but somebody stole her barrel and she died in poverty.

Ten years later, London cockney Bobby Leach survived his leap with broken jaw and kneecaps, only to die years later after slipping on a fruit peel in New Zealand. All that was found among the smithereens of barber Charlie Stevens' barrel was his right arm. A Greek cook went over with his pet turtle, but only the turtle got out alive. After the third fatal accident, in 1951, the province decided to make it an offence to go over the falls without a permit from the Niagara Parks Commission. Since then, several daredevils have gone over regardless. In 1985, a Florida bartender decorated his barrel with the words "Support Reagan". The group to try their luck in summer 1995 were fined $10,000.

whole river and falls area, swooping low around the Horseshoe.

Away from the hustle and hype, **Queen Victoria Park** is a delight for hikers, cyclists, picnickers—even cross-country skiers in winter, when the falls take on a much more romantic look, all the more so for being relatively deserted. In spring, the park gardens put on a magnificent show of daffodils, tulips, magnolias and roses, and diners in the park restaurant get a great view of the falls' night-time illuminations.

Niagara-on-the-Lake

A meandering 30-km riverside drive north along the lovely tree-lined **Niagara Parkway** takes you from the tumult of the tourist buses to the tranquillity of this old Loyalist bastion. The town, settled by refugees from the American Revolution in 1792 and briefly capital of Upper Canada, jealously preserves an image of a "British" way of life revisited by North American nostalgia. The main street, **Queen Street,** pays tribute to the Anglo-Saxon myth with its clock tower, white clapboard and red-brick houses, the grand Prince of Wales Hotel, tea shops serving buns and buttered scones, and the lovingly restored **Niagara Apothecary** (1866) displaying old-fashioned medicine jars in walnut cabinets under ornamental crystal gaslights.

On the quiet avenues off the main street, you can taste something of the genteel life in some delightful little boarding houses that supplement the usual hotels. They operate principally from April to October, when the town hosts the popular **Shaw Festival.** Works of George Bernard Shaw and other major playwrights are performed in the modern Festival Theatre (Wellington Street and Queen's Parade Road) with its pleasant garden for a cocktail between acts. A couple of smaller theatres put on musical comedies and light revues.

On the outskirts of town, **Fort George**, the British garrison on the Niagara frontier during the War of 1812, was destroyed by the Americans and restored in the 1930s. A rebuilt stockade of six earth and log bastions connected by a wooden palisade surrounds workshops, hospital, kitchens and the original 1797 stone powder house. Infantry and artillery drills are staged in the summer.

Apart from B.C.'s Okanagan Valley, the Niagara peninsula is Canada's only serious wine-growing area, not comparable with Bordeaux or Burgundy, but still respectable. At St. Davids, south-west of town, you can visit the Château des Charmes **winery** and taste for yourself.

⚜ Stratford

Situated in the heart of the peninsula, 2 hours' drive from Toronto, the town is well worth a visit for its celebrated **Stratford Festival** spanning the whole tourist season, from May to November. Since Tyrone Guthrie opened the festival in a tent in 1953, Shakespeare and other English classics like Sheridan and Marlowe are given pride of place. Their home is now the apron-staged **Festival Theatre**, while the Avon Theatre and Tom Patterson Theatre offer jazz and chamber music concerts as well as a chance to discover Canadian playwrights.

Every effort is made to sustain an Elizabethan atmosphere, with curtain times heralded by trumpeters in Renaissance doublet and hose. Picnic in **Queen's Park** and give your crumbs to the ducks and swans on Victoria Lake. A **Shakespearean Garden** displays the flowers mentioned by the Bard in his sonnets and plays.

Point Pelee National Park

At the southern end of the peninsula, indeed the southernmost point of the Canadian mainland, Point Pelee is one of the most distinctive of the country's nature reserves. It's on the same latitude as northern California or Rome and so endowed with a most un-Canadian climate and vegetation that offer a hospitable crossroads for 345 species of birds on their biannual migrations away from northern and southern winters.

"Bald point", as French explorers dubbed it, is the southern half of a 20-km sandspit jutting out into Lake Erie. Its terrain is a mixture of marshland, forest, meadows and sandy beaches. Beginning with a lookout tower for bird-watchers, a circular boardwalk takes you out onto the marshes to observe the flight of the redwing blackbird and purple martin, while bittern stay tucked away in the reeds. Look, too, for the pretty pink-blossomed swamp rose-mallow, unique to Point Pelee. Well-marked bicycle and hiking nature trails wind through the woods where you'll see hackberry, sassafras, sycamore, black walnut and red cedar, many of the trees draped with hanging vines reminiscent of the American Carolinas.

In the spring, the great sport is fishing for smelt during their spawning run, ending the day with a communal fish-fry on the beach. In September, even before the leaves turn, trees go bright orange with the wings of millions of Monarch butterflies on their way to Mexico.

At long last, peace for the Hurons at the Sainte-Marie mission.

LAKES HURON AND SUPERIOR

Ontario's playgrounds, weekend cottages and marinas hug the shores and islands of the upper Great Lakes, offering first-class resort hotel facilities. The more adventurous campers, hikers and canoers can explore the national and provincial parks for a taste of the northern interior's wilderness.

Georgian Bay

The bay forms practically a separate lake. These old stamping grounds of the Huron Indians (until they were decimated by Iroquois warriors and European disease) are now a popular weekend and summer destination for the families of tired Toronto businessmen.

The town of **Midland** is the centre of the Huron region. Its

Huronia Museum and the copy of a Huron village in Little Lake Park illustrate the simple lifestyle of the Indians before the arrival of the Jesuits in the 17th century. West of town, **Sainte-Marie among the Hurons** is a reconstruction of the Jesuit mission built in 1639. Today, besides some (real) Huron Indians, costumed students show you how the community functioned with priests, carpenters, gardeners and blacksmiths. It's worth beginning your visit with the half-hour documentary film to understand the dramatic fate of the mission.

It must be said that the Huron were less interested in conversion to Christianity than in the goods to be gained from the fur traders who followed the priests on this first French settlement in Ontario. But dealing directly with Europeans threatened the position of the rival Iroquois as middlemen between the Huron (and Algonquin) and the Dutch and British traders down in Albany, New York. The Iroquois killed thousands of Huron in all-out war, and two Jesuits, Jean de Brébeuf and Gabriel Lalemant, were tortured to death. To halt the Iroquois advance, the French community of 300 burned their own village and returned to Quebec.

The simple little **Church of St. Joseph** contains the tombs of the martyred missionaries. A **museum** outside the stockade depicts the life of the 17th-century French-Canadians, including the artefacts and birchbark canoes of the fur traders.

The dramatic landscapes of the **Georgian Bay Islands National Park**, a particular favourite of the Group of Seven, now attract fishermen, scuba divers and other water sports enthusiasts. The Bay's islands are said to number 30,000, if you include all the rocky outcrops and sandbanks with a clump of trees, and the park includes 59 of the most attractive.

Midland and Tobermory offer **boat cruises** and shuttle services out to individual islands. **Beausoleil Island**, off Honey Harbour just outside Midland, is the focus or launching pad of the islands park, very well equipped for camping (there are no restaurant facilities on any of the islands, so be sure to take your own supplies). The **Tobermory Islands** are renowned for their rock formations, most notably **Flowerpot Island** where tall limestone monoliths have been eroded into bizarre vase-like shapes.

Thunder Bay

For vacationers, the town strategically located on Lake Superior's north-west shore is a springboard to the national parks of Ontario's interior. But it's also worth taking a look first at the impressive **port** facilities of this western terminus of the St. Lawrence–Great Lakes Seaway which has given Thunder Bay its second name: the Lakehead. Freighters come 3,200 km inland from the Atlantic to take on grain shipments from the Prairie Provinces or bring other heavy cargo to all points west in both Canada and the U.S. Starting out from the centrally located North Marina, a **harbour cruise** takes you around the gigantic fortress-like grain silos for a close-up view of the ships in dock.

A longer cruise from the same marina follows the Kaministiquia River to **Old Fort William** (20 minutes by car), the handsomely reconstructed trading post of the Nor'Westers, intrepid rivals of the Hudson's Bay Company (see p. 22). Sheep graze the courtyard lawns, bread is still made in the bakery, and the *canteine* provides lusty country fare. In the company store, you'll see the kind of simple copper and pewter utensils and steel knives that were more precious than gold to the Ojibwa Indians bringing in their beaver pelts.

Just up the road, in its own provincial park providing a quiet natural setting that's a far cry from Niagara, is the beautiful **Kakabeka Falls**. A boardwalk takes you through the woods along the Kaministiquia River and across a bridge for a view of the falls from both sides. The cascade flows at its fullest in spring and autumn when the hydrostations don't slow it down. There are good facilities for camping and bathing.

Canoers and hikers really intent on getting away from civilization head two hours west of Thunder Bay along Highway 11 to the **Quetico Provincial Park**. This is the country through which the Nor'Westers' *coureurs de bois* paddled their way to the Indian trappers' remote camps, adopting the natives' lore for tackling the wilderness, including their snowshoes, toboggans and birchbark canoes. The Indians have been here for 9,000 years and have left their coloured pictographs of moose, caribou, bears and turtles etched in the granite cliffs.

The only road into the park leads to the Dawson Trail Campgrounds on **French Lake**—pleasant for a day's picnic and swimming. For longer stays, the information office provides detailed maps of Quetico's fantastic network of interlocking waterways. You can rent a canoe—no motor launches allowed—and fishing equipment (excellent pike, bass and trout) in the old mining and logging town of **Atikokan**.

OTTAWA

Like most national capitals created artificially to avoid favouring one established metropolis over another, Ottawa is the perennial butt of carping and jokes. It's true of Washington, of Brasília, of Canberra, and even more so in Canada where the very idea of a centralized federal government is so hotly contested by its independent-minded provinces. People rarely like government at the best of times, and when it's the town's main, almost exclusive "industry", they have a built-in adverse prejudice right there.

But Ottawa's third major source of income is nonetheless tourism, because the town is pleasant, offering a pretty setting of parks and waterways for its first-class museums and colourful monuments. The country's short history is epitomized by a skyline of solid Victorian parliamentary buildings and a bold modern architecture of office blocks and the new National Gallery. And the government machinery remains firmly in touch with its roots when in winter the bureaucrats skate and ski to work along the frozen Rideau Canal.

Accommodatingly situated on the border between Ontario and Quebec, Ottawa is a fully bilingual city, though most of the French-speaking community (and the best restaurants) now have their homes in Hull on the Quebec side of the Ottawa River.

Except for longer excursions, try to leave the car in the hotel parking lot and walk or take the bus. The complex system of one-way streets designed to avoid rather than to reach key government buildings, and the added confusion of curving rivers and canals, make downtown driving a harrowing business even for local citizens. One other point: in the absence of any clear logic in street numbering, it's important when noting an address to be sure you have the nearest cross-streets as well as the number of the building.

Parliament Area

Like their London mother from which they unashamedly take their architectural inspiration, the **Parliament Buildings** are an imposing neo-Gothic pile currently undergoing extensive renovation work. They dominate the Ottawa River from a bluff somewhat exaggeratedly known as Parliament Hill. As a counterpart to Westminster's Big Ben, the 302.5-ft **Peace Tower** with clocks on all four sides and a 53-bell carillon was built in front of the Centre Block as a monument to World War I. With the tower in scaffolding until late 1996, the observation deck is closed until further notice.

Guided tours take in the chambers of the Senate (in place of Britain's House of Lords) and the House of Commons. If you want to attend a debate, the tourist office (National Arts Centre, 65 Elgin Street) will advise you on how to get a permit. In the Centre Block, the handsome pine-panelled **Library of Parliament** miraculously survived the 1916 fire. Beneath the formidable Gothic rotunda, you'll see an imperial, almost goddess-like

---

Capital Assets?

A British journalist accompanying the Prince of Wales on a visit to Ottawa in the 1860s reported to his newspaper that the new government buildings were "admirably suited for lunatic asylums whenever the town is sufficiently prosperous to require them for that purpose." Ottawa has always had a hard time gaining respect.

It began life in the early 19th century as a lumber depot at the confluence of the Gatineau, Rideau and Ottawa rivers—very useful log-movers, with the Rideau waterfall providing hydraulic power for the sawmills. Lieutenant-Colonel John By made it his headquarters, Bytown, for constructing the Rideau Canal as a new strategic link between Montreal and Upper Canada, after the War of 1812 had revealed the vulnerability of the St. Lawrence River. Peace with the U.S. and improved roads soon made it obsolete for anything but pleasure cruises.

The ethnic and religious rivalries of Irish immigrant construction crews and an assortment of Anglo and French lumberjacks and fur

traders exploded regularly into riots. After a visit of the governor general in 1843, Protestant Orangemen left a symbolic arch of orange tiger lilies which the Catholics tore down rather than pass under on their way to Sunday mass. The ensuing riot left one dead and 50 badly injured. The authorities felt obliged to erect a boxing ring on Rideau Street to absorb the people's aggressivity.

All the more ironic, then, that this should be the capital the British recommended to Queen Victoria (with the aid of highly flattering watercolours) as a peaceful compromise avoiding the ethnic provocation of Toronto or Montreal. In keeping with its position on the border between French and English Canada, it chose for its new name, in place of the too English Bytown or anything remotely French, the neutral Ottawa, after a tribe of Algonquin Indians highly respected for their trapping. An important strategic consideration was its remoteness from the then still insecure American border— "Westminster in the wilderness", as contemporaries called it.

---

marble statue of Victoria surrounded by more mortal early Canadian prime ministers. Some of the latter's offices have been restored in the **East Block** (1872), which also survived the fire.

Switching its echoes from Westminster to Buckingham Palace, Parliament Hill offers in the summer at 10 a.m a daily half-hour **Changing of the Guard** by 135 soldiers of the Governor General's Foot Guards and Canadian Grenadier Guards. On summer evenings, the Parliament Buildings are illuminated by a sound and light show presenting a 45-minute history of Canada, in English or French.

Sparks Street Mall, first street in Ottawa to be paved and now the city's, indeed the country's, first traffic-free pedestrian zone, is a pleasant shopping area enlivened by street musicians and clowns and bordered by some first-class modern office buildings. Pride of place goes to the elegant 12-storey mirror-glass **Bank of Canada** (between Kent and Bank streets) by Arthur Erickson. The green patina of the building's copper skeleton is an artful homage to the copper roofs on the old Parliament Buildings. Inside is the Currency Museum (see p. 79).

On the vast three-sided Confederation Square—popularly known for its traffic congestion as "Confusion Square"—notice the great granite arch of the **National War Memorial** with its statues of 22 World War I soldiers and a horse-drawn cannon. Ironically, it was dedicated by George VI just three months before the outbreak of World War II. The square's bunker-like **National Arts Centre** houses the capital's ballet, opera and theatre, but it's the summer beer-garden overlooking the Rideau Canal that is the most popular attraction. Getting a federal government's priorities in proper perspective, one member of parliament bemoaned the cultural centre as "50 years ahead of its time—that's how long it'll take the taxpayers to meet the 500 per cent cost overrun." The formidable **Château Laurier**, an old railway hotel on the north side of the square, is built in the Renaissance castle style much favoured by the C.P.R and C.N.R for their luxury transcontinental hostelries.

Local citizens boast that the **Rideau Canal**, which stretches 202 km from the Ottawa River to Lake Ontario, qualifies in winter as "the world's longest skating rink". In summer, it offers delightful boat cruises and canoeing, or you can explore its banks with a rented bicycle.

"Hurry up with your picture, I have to get home for lunch."

On the edge of the parliamentary district, across the Rideau Canal, is **Byward Market** (one block east of Sussex Drive and north of Rideau Street). Since 1846 when it was a clearing house for nearby farmers, this has been the popular centre of town, meeting place for the non-politicos. In its jolly, well-restored state, only one of the market stalls dates as far back as 1867, but it retains much of its 19th-century atmosphere. Quite apart from the colourful stalls of fruit and vegetables, it's a great place for breakfast, and, like most places in the town, is open on Sundays.

Sussex Drive

This is the grand parade drive along the Ottawa River to the town's smartest residential neighbourhood, home of ministers and "Embassy Row".

The neo-Gothic **Basilica of Notre-Dame** (Sussex at Guigues) was born with the capital. The Catholic cathedral's steeples went up in 1858, though the whole church was not completed until 1890. Quebec sculptors Louis Philippe Hébert, Philippe Parizeau and Flavien Rochon carved the pulpit, choir stalls, organ loft and bas-reliefs.

Turn off on St. Patrick Street to drive through **Nepean Point** to where a statue of Samuel de Champlain, founder of Quebec, looks west along the Ottawa River with his Huron Indian scout. Here he still has the astrolabe which he lost on his explorations and which gave its name to the nearby **Astrolabe Amphitheatre**, attractive setting for summer open-air concerts.

Where the road crosses over the Rideau River and Green Island, look out for **Rideau Falls** pouring its double "curtain" (French *rideau*) of water into the Ottawa River. The current exhibit is a display of Canadian achievements and is open from June to October.

For Canadians, **24 Sussex Drive** has the same significance as 10 Downing Street for the British. This grey stone house hidden behind the greenery is the Canadian prime minister's residence. His neighbour, in **Rideau Hall** just along the road (1 Sussex Drive), is the Queen's representative, the governor general. Five rooms are available for viewing (July, August, weekends only) and the 88 acres of green parkland may be admired during outdoor walking tours. There are also summer outdoor concerts from Canada Day to the last Sunday in August.

The drive then circles around the immaculate gardens and fine mansions of **Rockcliffe Park**. The park's driveway takes you out to the **Rockcliffe Lookout** for a spectacular view of the

Ottawa River and the mouth of the Gatineau. In the **Royal Canadian Mounted Police Stables** at the north end of St. Laurent Boulevard, you can see some of the horse performing or training for the popular Musical Ride, except when they are absent on tour.

Museums

In its sparkling new premises on Sussex Drive opposite the Basilica of Notre-Dame, the **National Gallery of Canada** makes an enchanting half-day excursion all to itself. Designed by Moshe Safdie, famous for his Habitat homes in Montreal, its permanent exhibits include the largest collection of Canadian art in the world. Some of the works and collections on rotation are listed below but may not be on display during your visit. The airy glass and steel construction brings natural daylight flooding into the spectacular Great Hall and all the galleries. Facing Nepean Point Park is the terrace of the main restaurant, while a more casual lunch room looks out onto the lovely garden of the neighbouring War Museum (see p. 79).

European Collections. Among the most important works from the 14th to the 18th century are Simone Martini's *St. Catherine of Alexandria*, Cranach's *Venus*, Hans Baldung Grien's *Eve, the Serpent and Death*, Hans Memling's *Virgin, Christ and St. Anthony*, Bronzino's *Portrait of a Man*, Annibale Carracci's *Vision of St. Francis*, Poussin's *Landscape with a Woman Washing Her Feet*, Rubens' *Entombment of Christ*, Rembrandt's *Heroine from the Old Testament* and Chardin's *The Governess*.

The 19th-century exhibits include works by Turner, Constable, Pissarro, Monet, Degas and Cézanne. Klimt and James Ensor provide the transition to the 20th century, well represented by Matisse, Picasso, Braque and Francis Bacon.

Contemporary Art. The collections in which American artists come to the fore present works by Jackson Pollock, Barnett Newman, Kenneth Noland, the Pop Art of James Rosenquist, Andy Warhol and Claes Oldenburg, the Minimalist sculpture of Donald Judd and Dan Flavin, and Conceptualists like Solo Lewitt and Joseph Kosuth. The most important of contemporary Canadians here include Guido Molinari, Yves Gaucher and Michael Snow.

Canadian Collections. At the heart of this impressive array of works by Canadian artists is the reconstructed interior of the 19th century Rideau Street Convent Chapel. You should also look for Thomson's *Jack Pine*, A.Y. Jackson's *Red Maple,* Lawren

Harris's *North Shore, Lake Superior*, murals by Thomson, Arthur Lismer and J.E.H. Mac-Donald, and Emily Carr's *Indian Hut, Queen Charlotte Islands*. **Inuit Art** has some impressive sculpture, prints and drawings from the 1950s and '60s.

The **Photographs Collection** covers the history of the art from William Henry Fox Talbot through Eugène Atget, Walker Evans and August Sander to the

Tom Thomson's Jack Pine *was a major influence on the Group of Seven.*

contemporary work of Diane Arbus and Paul Diamond.

The august **Victoria Memorial Building** at Metcalfe and McLeod streets houses the **Canada Museum of Nature,** containing treasures uncovered by the Geological Survey of 1841, predating the foundation of Canada itself. The survey went as far as studying the uncharted country's palaeontology and anthropology, its climate, forestry and botany. (The anthropological exhibits are now in the Canadian Museum of Civilisation in Hull.) A new permanent exhibition includes The Viola MacMillan Mineral Gallery; another attraction is the **Dinosaur Court** devoted to the 75,000,000 year-old beasts excavated in Alberta.

The **National Museum of Science and Technology** (1867 St. Laurent Boulevard) is in the now consecrated style of science through fun and games. There are views of the heavens through a huge refracting telescope, do-it-yourself demonstrations of balance and optics, and a collection of antique cars and old train engines.

In a similar vein, the **National Aviation Museum** at Rockcliffe Airport traces the history of aviation through the early flying machines, bi- and triplanes, and the great fighters of two world wars. The exhibition includes the *Silver Dart*, the first plane flown in the British Empire, in 1909. In a country where remote, sparsely populated areas have made it more dependent than most on air transport, a special place is reserved for the sturdy little bushplanes used to cover the wilderness. About 45 aircraft are displayed in the museum while the rest are in open storage at the back of the building. Many of the wartime planes take to the skies again on Annual Aeronautical Day (1st July).

The **Canadian War Museum**, 330 Sussex Drive, starts with Indian warfare, including the battle prizes of scalps and skulls, and ends, we'd like to believe, with the Canadian involvement in the Korean War. Field Marshal Göring's armoured Mercedes Benz makes a nice latter-day battle prize. Weapons range from Indian clubs and tomahawks to the longer-range guided missiles of today's armed forces.

Outside the **Currency Museum** (Bank of Canada, 245 Sparks Street between Kent and Lyon) is a 3-ton stone "coin" from the Caroline Islands in the Pacific. The smaller stuff is inside, including the Indian currency of beads, wampum (black and white shells), beaver pelts and blankets, Inuit whales' teeth and the more familiar coinage and paper currency from colonial to modern times. Across the Alexander Bridge in Hull is the excellent **Canadian Museum of Civilisation,** with fascinating displays and artefacts tracing the history of the country, and temporary exhibitions on a range of related topics. The museum can be found at 100 Laurier Street.

Gatineau Park

A 20-minute drive across the Ottawa River into Quebec, but actually the most popular of excursions from the national capital, this 36,000-hectare park of lakes and woodland covers an escarpment with dramatic lookouts over the plains of the Ottawa Valley. It's named after the French hunter Nicolas Gatineau who first explored it, and its evergreen and deciduous forests are still the home of an abundant wildlife.

Go hiking or biking on well-planned nature trails (details can be obtained from the visitors centre). Besides swimming at five public beaches, you can rent canoes and rowing boats for fishing on Philippe and La Pêche lakes. In the district of **Kingsmere,** visit the estate where Wil-

liam Lyon Mackenzie King spent his last years. As well as exploring the occult—he spoke to his departed mother through a crystal ball—Canada's longest-serving prime minister liked to collect "ruins" on his many world travels. Among others, you'll find in his gardens pieces of London's House of Commons, brought back after the Blitz of World War II.

EASTERN ONTARIO

The narrow arm of territory between Ottawa and the St. Lawrence River lies at the historic heart of Upper Canada. This was the home of early Loyalist settlers. Ships were built here to navigate the Great Lakes, and later it became the site for the key section of the St. Lawrence Seaway, linking Montreal to Lake Ontario.

Upper Canada Village

Here, the two strands of the region's history come together in the meticulous recreation of a pioneering village, perhaps the best of the country's many historical showpieces. The homes of the region's first settlers had to be moved here, east of Morrisburg, when their original location was flooded in the digging of the St. Lawrence Seaway. Start your visit by climbing the **Signal Tower** from which you get an overall view. In a peaceful, green canalside setting disturbed only by cheeky Canada geese, notoriously loud honkers, you'll find authentic pre-1867 buildings, from the simple timbered sawmill or old schoolhouse to the sophisticated brick-built **Crysler Hall** in the Palladian style favoured by colonial land-

There's one for almost everybody among the Thousand Islands in the St. Lawrence River.

81

owners from Ontario to Alabama. Crysler was a farmer on whose land an important battle was fought in the War of 1812, marked by a monument beside the village.

Period-costumed artisans demonstrate the crafts of the village, weaving, bread-baking, ploughing and sowing. In the colonial setting of **Willard's Hotel**, you can enjoy a home-cooked hot meal or salad lunch.

Kingston

Beautifully located on Lake Ontario at the head of the St. Lawrence River, the town gets its charm more from its universities and silvery-grey historic houses than from its federal and provincial prisons. Originally a trading post for the French and Indians, Kingston became a shipbuilding naval base in the War of 1812. **Fort Henry**, now spruced up by nicely enacted parades, was built in 1832 as the main military stronghold of Upper Canada. The fort never fired a shot in anger, but you can watch the daily 19th-century infantry drills during the summer (from 21 May to 3 September), with the Commandant's Parade at 2 p.m.

For a few years in the 1840s, its strategic position made Kingston capital of pre-Confederation Canada, and the sturdy, pillared **City Hall** with its lofty lanterned dome pays due homage to an illustrious past. Behind, on **Market Square,** the Saturday market attracts the best of Ontario's fruit and vegetables and the most brazen of the local artists and musicians.

Thousand Islands

Reached most easily from Kingston, this archipelago of in fact 1,800 islands is strung out along the St. Lawrence River for nearly 80 km. You can go fishing, sailing or lie back and enjoy a luxury cruise (5–7 days) around the islands aboard the *Empress* steamboat.

The island scenery is another painter's delight—the dark green of the spruces and silver birches against grey and pink granite outcrops. Millionaires such as songwriter Irving Berlin or cosmetic queen Helena Rubinstein have made this their playground with hideaway mansions known as "cottages". One that escapes that euphemism is **Boldt Castle,** the kind of Gothic folly that magnates liked to dabble in earlier this century. In this case, it was George Boldt, the German owner of New York's Waldorf Astoria Hotel. He built it for his wife but she died before it was finished, and it was abandoned as a vast empty fortress, like those that Boldt admired in similar splendid ruin back home in the Rhine Valley.

QUEBEC

If—oh, happy dream—all the old ethnic rivalries could be set aside, most Canadians would acknowledge that Quebec is not only the "original" Canada of the first European settlement, but also the province that most comprehensively encompasses within its borders the world's image of this huge country. To begin with, it is itself huge: it could contain, according to your taste, three Frances or seven Britains. Most of it—two-thirds of the area—is forest. The north is coniferous, serving the province's important pulp and paper industry, the south deciduous, with the maple of the national flag providing delicious syrup, and the ash, oak and beech that blaze into crimson, amber and gold in autumn.

There aren't as many beavers as in the great days of the fur trade, but still enough to fell a few trees around the resort cottages in the Laurentian Mountains north of Montreal. Deer and moose abound for the hunters, further north herds of caribou and, up towards the Arctic Circle, a few polar bears, too.

Where it's not forest, city or the farmland established by the *habitants* of the St. Lawrence Valley and the Eastern Township Loyalists, it's water, water everywhere. The mighty St. Lawrence River and Seaway link the Atlantic Ocean to the Great Lakes. Gigantic dams harness the water's hydroelectric power north on James Bay, east on the Manicouagan River. Lakes and streams shimmer with salmon, trout, and pike.

As you travel from bilingual Montreal to New France's old capital Quebec City and the resolutely French-speaking farm villages along the St. Lawrence and around the Gaspé Peninsula, have a thought for local patriotic sensibility. While the Inuit and Indians did get there a few thousand years before them, the Québécois can justly claim to be co-founders of the Canadian nation. Abandoned by what many still call the "damned French" *(maudits français),* they felt that they alone had earned the name of *canadiens,* and that their British conquerors usurped it. As a tribute to their own past courage, there is both pride and resentment in the Québécois motto *Je me souviens* (I Remember). It was they who made the first and hardiest effort to hew a modern living out of this hard land. Like colonials everywhere, their missionaries sometimes brought more religion, their traders more alcohol and their soldiers more guns than the natives really needed. But the Québécois understood the importance of learning from the Indians how best to handle the Canadian wilderness. Fur-trading *coureurs de bois* settled down with Indian wives, and today more than a few Québécois proudly trace their ancestry back to Indians with a tell-tale birthmark on the hip, high cheekbones and long sleek black hair.

Outside Montreal, you can't assume everyone speaks English. Many make it a point of pride not to, until you've at least paid them the courtesy of a *Bonjour.* By Quebec provincial law, public signs are all in French, and so we will often give you here, beside the English names, the French version as it appears on maps and signposts.

MONTREAL

This great metropolis is built on an island, at the confluence of the Ottawa and St. Lawrence rivers. Second in population now to Toronto, it remains a sprawling city of cosmopolitan neighbourhoods, each a delight to stroll around but best reached by taxi, bus or the excellent Métro subway, where the trains whoosh along on rubber tyres. Given the daytime traffic snarls and usual big-city parking problems, keep your car for out-of-town trips.

⚡ Mount Royal

For an overall view of the city, start with a bracing walk up the slopes of the charming **Mount Royal Park** *(Parc du Mont-Royal)*. Follow the footpath and stairs from the end of Peel Street or a shorter route from the Chemin Remembrance car park. Perhaps the pleasantest way is to take a leisurely ride with one of

the bus tours which leave from Dominion Square.

Known with characteristic local irony as *la Montagne* (the Mountain), the hillock was spotted by Jacques Cartier on his historic journey up the St. Lawrence River in 1535 and named Mont Réal in homage to his king François I.

From the massive timber and stone **Chalet de la Montagne** or the steel cross at the summit (illuminated at night), you look out over the river flowing from the Lac des Deux Montagnes past the city on its north-easterly journey

---

Do You Speak Joual?

However good you think your French French is, Canadian French may hold some surprises for you, quite apart from its distinctive accent. The French of the Québécois has become a colourful combination of the language they spoke back in the 17th century, a vocabulary heavily influenced by their American neighbours, and some picturesque concoction all their own. The patois of the working class is known as joual, *after the pronunciation of the French word for horse,* cheval.

Here are a few sources of confusion. Char *is not a tank, as in French French, but an ordinary car. Its fuel is not* essence, *but* gaz *(like American* gas*). Nothing to do with heat,* chauffer *means to drive*

(derived from chauffeur*). A tow-away zone is* zone de touage. *And in this context, don't call a* dépanneur *expecting a car mechanic; in Quebec it's a grocery shop open after normal shopping hours.*

At meal times, remember that breakfast is déjeuner, *lunch is* dîner *and dinner is* souper. *Fried eggs are rather prettily* œufs au miroir. *You don't have to rack your brain for draught beer, it's simply* draffe, *but* liqueur *is just a gassy soft drink.* Bleuets *are blueberries, not cornflowers.*

American borrowings are sometimes direct, like le truck, *sometimes literal translations that greatly amuse the French, like* bas-culotte *for panty hose, or* bienvenue *(welcome) in perpetual reply to your thanks.*

*The uphill part of Mount Royal Park
is more fun if you have a horse
doing all the work.*

to the Atlantic. Montrealers conveniently twist the compass by considering the St. Lawrence as "south" of the city; the roads parallel to the river are divided into "east" and "west" sectors by the Boulevard St-Laurent. Down by the port are the low stone buildings of Old Montreal *(Vieux Montréal)*. The concrete, steel and glass towers of the modern city cluster around Boulevard R-Lévesque which runs parallel to the river. At the far end, Jacques-Cartier Bridge links Montreal Island to the Expo '67 site on St. Helen's Island *(Ile Ste-Hélène)* and over to the "southern" shore. Victoria Bridge spans the St. Lawrence to your right.

South-west of Mount Royal, on the slopes of the smaller hill of Westmount, are the grand villas and mansions of Montreal's old Anglo-Canadian élite. North and west of the park are many of the city's ethnic neighbourhoods and the smarter French-speaking township of Outremont. On the clearest days, you may spot the Laurentian Mountains to the north-east and the Green Mountains across the U.S. border in Vermont.

Landscaped by Frederick Law Olmsted, designer of New York's Central Park, Mount

Royal is a popular refuge from the city bustle: picnics in the summer, tobogganing and skiing in the winter, with the little **Beaver Lake** *(Lac des Castors)* for sailing model boats (or skating). A stroll around the lake is the perfect way to capture a sense of the town's ethnic diversity. On the park benches, you may hear gossip not only in French and English, but Italian, Greek, Yiddish and Russian.

🏃 Old Montreal

Between Rue St-Antoine and the port and flanked by Rue McGill and Rue Berri, this is the site of Maisonneuve's original settlement of Ville-Marie (Métro Champ-de-Mars). All but a few stones of the 18th-century city ramparts have gone, but many historic houses have been restored to evoke some of the flavour of New France.

The colourful, tree-lined square of **Place Jacques-Cartier** makes a good point at which to start your walking tour (unless you prefer to ride in a horse-drawn *calèche* available here for hire). You can map out your itinerary over coffee at one of the many pleasant sidewalk cafés. Once a fruit and vegetable market, the cobblestone square remains a favourite venue for flower-vendors and itinerant artists. Notice how the old stone

87

buildings were designed to beat the harsh winters with tall, steep-sloping roofs to keep snow and ice from accumulating.

Across the Rue Notre-Dame, the 19th-century **Hôtel de Ville** (City Hall) is built in the imposing style of the French Renaissance. It was from the balcony beneath the clock in 1967 that General de Gaulle delivered his incendiary cry of "*Vive le Québec libre!*", warming the hearts of local separatists. A local English-language newspaper spluttered that this intervention in Canadian affairs was the act of "an elephant run amok". The general was not intimidated by the **statue of Lord Horatio Nelson** watching him from the top of Place Jacques-Cartier. Montreal's oldest monument was somewhat provocatively erected in 1809, just four years after the British admiral's devastating defeat of the French at Trafalgar.

Diagonally opposite the Hôtel de Ville on Rue Notre-Dame, the **Château Ramezay** was home of the French governor Claude de Ramezay from 1705 to 1724. It passed successively into the hands of the French West Indies Trading Company (to store its spices), the British and, during their brief occupation of the city in 1775, the American generals Richard Montgomery and Benedict Arnold. Benjamin Franklin stayed there during his fruitless attempt to win Quebec over to the American cause. After years of neglect, the château has been restored and transformed into a **museum** showing a more comfortable side of frontier life in New France with a grand colonial kitchen in the basement, and the nice added touch of magnificent carved mahogany panelling imported from the old trading company's French offices. Iroquois clothes and artefacts give a hint of what life was like outside the stockade.

The **Rue Bonsecours** is one of the principal historic residential streets leading from Rue Notre-Dame towards the Vieux Port (Old Port). The **Maison Papineau** (No. 440), distinguished by its double row of gabled garrets in the roof, dates back to 1785. It is the family home of the controversial 19th-century politician Louis-Joseph Papineau, leader of the militant *patriotes* but also cautious protector of his seigneurial property (see p. 22). In 1837, the house nearly burned down in a violent riot, and British soldiers had to come to Papineau's rescue. He fled to the countryside and did not take part in the subsequent insurrection.

On the corner of Rue St-Paul, the older **Maison du Calvet** was built in 1770 by a prominent Huguenot merchant. As a Protestant, Pierre du Calvet was appointed by the British justice of the peace but then ended up in jail himself for selling supplies and information to the American invaders. With its broad chimney, fine-grained limestone frames around the doors and gracefully tapered casement windows, the house is one of the more handsome architectural specimens of the French colonial era. The sturdy interior of wide, rough-hewn floorboards and massive pinewood roofbeams is fitted out from the Montreal Museum of Fine Arts with antique Quebec furniture, rugs, lanterns, clocks and porcelain appropriate to the life of a wealthy 18th-century businessman. A framed copy of the bilingual *Quebec Gazette*, dating from 1786, suggests that colonials of the New World had an uncommon interest in the more arcane news of international events in the Old World. The house is now a Bed and Breakfast hotel and is not open to general view.

Since 1772, the church of **Notre-Dame-de-Bonsecours** stands on the site of a chapel built for the colony's first schoolteacher, Marguerite Bourgeois, but destroyed by fire. It was she and three young woman companions who brought a civilizing influence to the harshness of the beleaguered settlement. Acting as both teachers and nurses, they also took charge of marriageable girls known as the *filles du Roi*, the "King's daughters", who were in fact daughters of peasants and poor artisans shipped over from France as wives for bachelor farmers and fur traders. In the 19th century, Notre-Dame-de-Bonsecours became the "Sailors' Chapel", to which survivors of shipwrecks brought model ships they had carved as offerings of thanksgiving. The models still hang from the ceiling, lit up now by tiny electric bulbs. Notice how the *trompe l'œil* painting on the low arched ceiling aspires to turn the little church into a lofty Gothic cathedral. If you climb the church tower you will get a good view of Vieux Montréal and the harbour.

Ugly old warehouses are being progressively demolished along the **Vieux Port** at the foot of Place Jacques-Cartier to make way for a summer festival of concerts and shows, with a mixture of jazz, pop and classical music as well as mime and dance. Some have been refurbished as cafés or to house a lively flea market. Take a walk along the port to Pointe à Callières where the Ville-Marie settlers first landed. An obelisk on the nearby **Place Royale** commemorates their adventure. The **Musée d'archéologie et d'histoire de Montréal** at the Pointe has a multi-media show and many fascinating exhibits.

The Rue St-Sulpice takes you over the **Place d'Armes,** close to the site of the first French battles with the Iroquois. Today it serves as a visual link between the historic old town of the pioneers and the new city of commerce and industry. In the middle is a **statue of Maisonneuve,** looking like a musketeer and brandishing the royal French fleur-de-lys flag that inspired the Quebec provincial flag of today. The 19th-century neo-Gothic **Notre-Dame Basilica** was designed by James O'Donell, an Irish Protestant New Yorker so inspired by his assignment that he converted to Catholicism. The great bell in the west tower (called *Le Gros Bourdon*) weighs 12 tons (11,240 Kg), but electricity now replaces the 12 men needed to clang it. The garishly opulent interior was the work of a Québécois, Victor Bourgeau. **Our Lady of the Sacred Heart Chapel,** behind the main altar, unites modern and traditional religious art in a more intimate setting for marriages and memorial services. A little **museum** displays church sculpture and painting, notably some almost surreal works by Pierre-Adolphe-Arthur Guindon, a Sul-

Notre-Dame's lavishly gilded altar was designed to rouse Quebec's flagging religious fervour.

pician monk. Next to the church is the **Seminary of St-Sulpice,** Montreal's oldest surviving edifice, built in 1683 to lead the missionary work among the Iroquois. It also boasts North America's oldest public clock (1701).

The Place d'Armes is enclosed on three sides by modern buildings, including the huge Post Office tower, while opposite Notre-Dame stands the venerable **Bank of Montreal.** The black marble and brass of its monumental entrance hall impose a pious appreciation of Canada's oldest banking institution. The statue of *Patria* is dedicated to the fallen of World War I. Take a peep, too, around the grand Exchange Room, awe-inspiring relic of the days when Canadian money was in the hands of august gentlemen, before they handed it over to those slick young Golden Boys of Toronto. A little banking museum shows the way it used to be, complete with a teller's window in the style of the bank's foundation in 1817.

Back down by the river, **Place d'Youville,** named after a lady who established here the charitable order of the Grey Nuns, offers a quieter, more romantic end to your tour of Vieux Montréal. The **Youville Stables** *(Ecuries d'Youville)* are an enchanting collection of early 19th-century grey-stone gabled buildings now containing restaurants and offices looking out onto a peaceful garden. Until recently, the courtyard made a lovely setting for plays and recitals in the summer. The ''stables'' were in fact nothing more romantic than a potassium warehouse, but they did for a time serve as a garage for horse-carriages. Next to the stables is an old red-brick fire station transformed into the **Montreal History Centre** *(Centre d'histoire de Montréal),* presenting an audiovisual documentary history of the city.

Downtown

The nucleus of downtown Montreal is located between Boulevard R-Lévesque and Sherbrooke Street running parallel to the river, bounded by Guy and St-Denis streets. It's an ongoing ferment of construction—bold new office skyscrapers, cultural complexes and shopping centres, crowding in on a die-hard bunch of old churches, museums and all-night delicatessens.

Start at **Square Dorchester,** where the horse-drawn *calèches* wait (they are also rather nicely known as *hippomobiles*). Artists and flower-vendors sell their wares around Henry Moore's sculpture of a *Reclining Nude* and more austere statues of Scottish poet Robert Burns and Canadian prime ministers Wilfrid Laurier and John Mac-

Donald. The Sun Life skyscraper, constructed in 1918, is the city's oldest and long held the distinction of being the tallest building in the British Empire. The tourist office at 1001 Square Dorchester (second entrance at 1010 Ste Catherine west) deals with tourism for the whole province; the office for Montreal only is at Place Jacques-Cartier. Both are open all year round.

North-east along Boulevard R-Lévesque is the Roman Catholic cathedral of Montreal, something of a visual oddity, at least for European visitors. The cathedral of **Marie-Reine-du-Monde** (Mary, Queen of the World) is a 19th-century half-size replica of St. Peter's Basilica in Rome. Half-size but still massive enough—inside, the nave is 328 ft long, transept 220 ft and the vault of the dome 250 ft high. Beneath that dome, over the high altar, is another replica of St. Peter's: Bernini's celebrated gilded bronze canopy. Unfortunately, there is nothing to match Bernini's great square to give you a proper perspective, and the church is dwarfed by the huge Queen Elizabeth Hotel and the Sun Life skyscraper.

The new gigantism continues with **Place Ville-Marie,** designed in an interesting cruciform shape by I.M. Pei, Affleck & Associates; it is dominated by both the Queen Elizabeth, Canadian National Railway's Central Station and the soaring Royal Bank.

But Place Ville-Marie is, above all, the starting point of Montreal's vast **underground city,** which acts as an ecological punchline to the joke of a Quebec winter. In self-defence against five or six months of ice, snow and slush, 150,000 pedestrians frequent a complete alternative city of shops, cinemas, nightclubs, restaurants, cafés. Hotel residents can spend a whole night out on the town in the winter months without overcoat or galoshes. And it's almost as popular on a sweltering day in July. Some 29 km of subterranean galleries (linked by Métro) stretch across the city, taking in Place Ville-Marie and Place Bonaventure, Les Terrasses, Place des Arts and Complexe Desjardins, and even passing under the St. Lawrence River to the suburb of Longueuil situated on the south shore.

Back above ground, **Rue Ste-Catherine** is the city's main shopping thoroughfare—department stores, cinemas, travel agencies, delicatessens and bars —more popular than chic, but always lively. At the corner of University Street the Anglican cathedral of **Christ Church**

The soaring towers of the Royal Bank were the work of I.M. Pei.

(1859) is a classic piece of elegant English Gothic—take a look inside at the fine stone sculpture on the high altar.

Crescent Street, with neighbouring Mountain and Bishop streets, is one of Montreal's more fashionable boutique and bistro areas. The Victorian stone row houses have escaped demolition. They have been lovingly refurbished and brightly painted for conversion into off-beat shops, art galleries and bars for the singles crowd.

They make an appropriate transition from Ste-Catherine to the elegance of **Sherbrooke Street**. With the Museum of Fine Arts (see p. 102) near the intersection of Crescent Street, Sherbrooke is the town's main "gallery row", where high-priced antique, jewellery, silverware and oriental carpet shops mingle. Even if you're not staying there, the ritzy Ritz-Carlton Hotel makes a fine rendezvous for a restful or bracing cocktail in mid-sightseeing. Opposite the McCord Museum of local history (see p. 103), **McGill University** is Montreal's internationally renowned English-speaking university. Founded in the early 19th century by a Scottish fur trader, James McGill, and especially respected for its engineering and medicine faculties, it has a student enrolment of 15,000. In 1969, Québécois separatists staged violent but unsuccessful demonstrations to have it transformed into a French-speaking institution. (The city's other English-speaking college is Concordia, while the Université de Montréal and the Université du Québec à Montréal are both French-speaking).

Between Maisonneuve and R.-Lévesque boulevards, art and commerce come together at the **Place des Arts** and Complexe Desjardins. The centre comprises a concert hall, two theatres, a recital room, and a new room for music or theatre. At the **Salle Wilfrid-Pelletier**, home of the Montreal Symphony Orchestra, the elegant tone of the whole complex is set in the foyer decorated with Aubusson tapestries and sculptures in bronze, mahogany, aluminium and ceramics. Notice above the concert hall doors the soapstone carvings of the Inuit sculptor, Yununkpuk.

Across Rue Ste-Catherine, you pass through the imposing glass portals of the attractive multi-level shopping centre of **Complexe Desjardins**, opened in 1976 during the grand building spree of the Montreal Olympic Games. With waterfalls and fountains playing among trees and shrubbery, local architects La Haye-Ouellet and Blouin have created a fascinating environment for the myriad terraces, balconies, mezzanines and a sunken plaza. A plaza lunch is a great attraction for shoppers and office-workers. Most of the latter come from the adjoining government agencies and conference centres of the Complexe Guy-Favreau, which in turn is linked to the equally huge Palais des Congrès.

Montreal's Neighbourhoods

From a local point of view, Vieux Montréal is a tourist attraction for the landmarks of the city's historical beginnings, while downtown is for business and special nights out. But the real colour and spice of the people's everyday life is to be found in their neighbourhoods.

And you'll find in the architecture the missing links between the French-inspired homes of Vieux Montréal and the international anonymity of the city centre's 20th-century skyscrapers. While the bourgeoisie's red-brick or stone houses are clearly inspired by Georgian and Victorian London and grander residences by the country houses and châteaux of continental Europe, the working-class row houses with outside iron staircases leading to upper floors (thus saving space inside) are a more characteristic Montreal feature.

Almost a neighbourhood all to itself, **Boulevard St-Laurent** used to mark the "border" between the Anglo-Canadians to the west and the French-Canadians to the east. Anglos call it "the Main" and French-Canadians make a nice—and rare—compromise with "*la Main*". The neighbourhood lines have blurred in recent years, but the Main stays appropriately neutral, a veritable United Nations of Italian, Greek, Spanish, Polish, Jewish, Arab and Japanese speciality shops, grocery stores, delicatessens and cafés. Gourmets make a special pilgrimage down a little side-street to Waldman's **fish market**.

French-speaking students from the Université du Québec à Montréal meet in cafés, bistros and bookshops around **Rue St-Denis**. Here and around the tree-shaded **Square St-Louis**, nicely restored or equally nicely battered Victorian gingerbread mansions and iron-staircased row houses fight a picturesque rearguard action against the encroachment of the modern red-brick blocks of the university. At the west end of the square, **Rue Prince-Arthur** has been transformed into a pleasant tile-paved pedestrian mall of boutiques and restaurants with good Greek and Italian cuisine. The street is also one of the town's livelier night-time hangouts for jazz and folk music.

West of Boulevard St-Laurent, squeezed out by the urban redevelopment around the Complexe Guy-Favreau and Palais

95

des Congrès, the compact little **Chinatown** huddles into a six-block area around Rue de la Gauchetière. It's peopled by descendants of the valiant labourers who helped build the Canadian Pacific Railway.

Seek out Montreal's **Little Italy** north of Mount Royal around the **Jean-Talon Market** on the Place du Marché du Nord (Métro Jean-Talon). The best trattorias in town are here, blessedly not the most expensive. The raucous market gives a distinctively Italian flavour to the fruit and vegetables of the Quebec countryside—perhaps it's the imported Parma hams, salami and pecorino cheeses that you'll also find here for your picnic.

The Greeks, some 47,450 strong, have mostly chosen the area around the **Avenue du Parc,** east of Outremont, for their cafés and *taverna.* When ordering that delicious coffee, remember not to call it Turkish.

With second- and third-generation prosperity, most of the Jews have moved on from the **Rue St-Urbain** neighbourhood made famous by the writings of Mordecai Richler (*The Apprenticeship of Duddy Kravitz*) to

make way gradually for an equally colourful Portuguese community. A nearby monument of Jewish folklore that no amount of urban upheavals can seem to budge is the ever-crowded **Schwartz's Delicatessen** on "the Main". Assimilating more easily with the Anglo community—only Protestant schools accepted their children—Eastern European Jews have "grad-

You can't help smiling at local patriotic feeling, large-size or small.

uated'' to wealthy Westmount or emigrated, again, to Toronto. French-speaking Jews, more recent arrivals from North Africa, have settled in middle-class Outremont.

On the north side of Mount Royal, beyond the Chemin de la Côte-Ste-Catherine, the handsome villas of **Outremont** make up the favoured neighbourhood of the French-Canadian bourgeoisie, in fact an independent township situated within Montreal's city borders. Originally an Anglo stronghold, part of it is still known even among French-speakers as Upper-Outremont, family home of that splendidly ambiguous French-Canadian, prime minister Pierre Elliott Trudeau. The ''lower'' part of this independent township has a breezy street-life, especially among the sidewalk cafés on **Rue Bernard.**

And where have all the Anglos gone? Many of the upper-middle-class variety are holding out in **Westmount**. This bastion of the old Montreal élite of British origin became a prime target for the more violent members of the separatist *Front de libération du Québec*, who in the 1960s set off bombs in Westmount's mailboxes. Those not put off by this can still be seen in tweeds and cavalry twill, walking their dogs around **Summit Park**, where the Belvedere affords a fine view of

the city. Head for the tree-lined Summit Road, Summit Crescent and Summit Circle and you'll spot their ivy-covered mansions and grey-stone turreted châteaux half-concealed behind trees and shrubbery at the top of a grassy slope. The architecture here is a wonderful compendium of French Romanesque, German Gothic and Italian Renaissance. **Westmount Square** gives you a sharp but not inelegant jolt back into the 20th century with the black steel and glass office buildings of Mies van der Rohe.

Dominating the skyline beyond Westmount on the Côte-des-Neiges, **St. Joseph's Oratory** *(Oratoire St-Joseph)* receives up to 2 million Catholic pilgrims each year. The huge sanctuary, which holds 10,000 worshippers, commemorates the healing powers of Brother André. Born Alfred Bessette in 1845, one of a poor Québécois family of 12 children, Brother André was gatekeeper at the monastic Congregation of the Holy Cross. He administered to the sick in a small wooden chapel that he himself erected; it is still standing near the transept of the present oratory. Over a million faithful attended his funeral in 1937. His tomb is in the crypt. The best time to enjoy the bright and airy simplicity of the oratory's modern interior is at the Sunday organ recitals at 11 a.m.

Olympic Park

Located east of downtown opposite Maisonneuve Park (Métro Pie-IX), the complex of sports facilities built for the 1976 Olympic Games is an eloquent monument to the visions of grandeur that characterized Mayor Jean Drapeau. After the sweeping (some would say devastating) and still unfinished downtown redevelopment and the ambitious construction on the St. Lawrence River for Expo '67, the Olympic Park was to be the apotheosis of his "new Montreal". As you can see on one of the daily guided tours, the result is as grandiose in design as it has been ruinous in cost, to the continuing chagrin of local taxpayers with long memories and short bank balances.

Centrepiece is the mammoth **Olympic Stadium**, seating 70,000 spectators for the home games of the Montreal Expos baseball team and rock'n'roll concerts. At the end of the '80s, finishing touches were still being added to French architect Roger Taillibert's great concrete oval, its ingenious sliding roof and the huge tower linking the stadium to the **swimming complex**. The latter has no less than half a dozen pools, from the regulation Olympic-size racing pool to a scuba pool 50 ft deep. (Montreal's legendary ice hockey team, the Canadiens, plays at The Forum, 2313 Rue Ste-Catherine-Ouest.)

One of the most exciting attractions in Montreal is the **Biodôme,** a highly original museum devoted to the environment. It has recreated four ecosystems: a tropical forest (with over 1,000 fish, amphibians, reptiles, birds and mammals), a Laurentian forest (with conifer woods and a beaver lake), the St. Lawrence marine environment (a granite basin holding 2.5 million litres of water with a variety of marine life) and a polar region.

Beside the Olympic Park across Sherbrooke Street are the city's **Botanical Gardens.** This delightful oasis of greenery boasts some 26,000 species of plants and trees from all over the world, lovingly tended to resist the rigours of the Quebec climate. A miniature railway takes you around the gardens. Among the highlights are magnificent orchids and cacti in the greenhouses and an exquisite arboretum of Japanese bonsai.

St. Lawrence River

After years of hiding the river behind a bleak expanse of warehouses, factories and railway tracks, Montreal has opened up its waterfront, more recently with the music festivals and flea market of the Vieux Port, but largely at the earlier instigation of that much maligned Mayor Drapeau.

Expo '67 provided the major

breakthrough with the choice of the river's **Ile Ste-Hélène** as the principal site for the international pavilions. Permanent exhibitions in the Biosphere (on the St. Lawrence and the Great Lakes) are open daily from June to September (10 a.m.–8 p.m.).

In the middle of the island, close to where the French army burned its flags in Montreal's military capitulation to the British in 1760, the **D.M. Stewart Museum** is a restoration of the fort commissioned by the Duke of Wellington 60 years later. The military drills and parades staged there in the summer by uniformed students pay appropriate homage to both French and British tradition (in fact Scottish, since the soldiers are Fraser Highlanders). The museum displays ship models, maps, navigational instruments and utensils and Canada's weapons and uni-

forms from the 17th century to World War II.

Beyond Jacques Cartier Bridge, **La Ronde** amusement park plays every imaginable ultramodern variation on the swings and roundabouts of a country fair. Put the kids on the Gyrotron whirligig or Aquapark waterslide and watch them from the beer garden.

A bridge (leading from the Ste-Hélène Métro station)

Helter-skelter at La Ronde, and Habitat's inspired modulated madness.

crosses over to the **Ile Notre-Dame**. This artificial island built from landfill dredged for canal construction has been embellished by **Les Floralies** flower park in the centre of a circuit for Grand Prix motor racing. On the island's southern tip, beyond the

Victoria Bridge, you can climb an observation tower for a view of the highly impressive **St. Lambert Lock,** a key point on the great St. Lawrence Seaway. Alternatively, the **Casino de Montréal** offers a wide variety of entertainment and is open to guests over 18 from 11 a.m. to 3 a.m. Smart dress should be worn.

From the Cité du Havre north of Victoria Bridge, the controversial apartment complex of **Habitat,** designed by the Israeli-born architect Moshe Safdie for Expo '67, provides residents with a grandstand view of the river and its islands. What looks to some like the aftermath of a child's tantrum among its building blocks is on closer inspection an artful composition of 354 pre-cast concrete boxes (originally hoisted into place by crane) to create 158 homes of various sizes and combinations.

To see the river from the river, take a **harbour cruise** from Quai Victoria, the northernmost wharf in Vieux Montréal, at the foot of Rue Berri. Romantic variations include the Sunset Cruise, Love Boat Cruise and the many dinner-dance cruises on offer.

For the more sporting breed, rafting expeditions also start out from Quai Victoria to shoot the famous **Lachine Rapids.** By lowering the river level, the seaway has made them a little less "rapid" than in the canoeing days of the fur traders, but they're still good for a thrill or two in the very solid rafts of today, with waterproof clothing provided. You can also rent a bicycle for a pleasant ride along the **Lachine Canal,** dug in 1825 and deepened for the seaway in 1959. In winter, it makes a great skating rink.

Museums

The most important of Montreal's many museums is its **Museum of Fine Arts** (*Musée des Beaux Arts*), 1379 Sherbrooke Street West. It has an honourable collection of European artists, including El Greco, Rubens, Hans Memling, Cranach and Poussin, and the British 18th-century masters, Reynolds, Gainsborough, Raeburn, Romney and Hogarth. The moderns include Picasso and Giacometti.

But it's worth devoting most of your time here to the excellent **Canadian galleries.** In the 19th-century section, look out for the imposing, if rather severe, classical portraits of Antoine-Sébastien Plamondon (1802–95) and the markedly gentler works of his Québécois student and rival Théophile Hamel (1817–70).

Mah-Min or *The Feather* is a dramatic study of an Assiniboine Indian chief in Manitoba by Paul Kane (1810–71). This Torontonian born in County Cork, Ireland, travelled all over the continent to gather a visual record, at times somewhat romanticized, of Canada's Indians. His contemporary, Amsterdam-born Cornelius Krieghoff (1815–72), concentrated on the Quebec peasantry and landscapes, as shown by *Montmorency Falls in Winter* (currently in storage).

The dazzling *Village Street, West Indies*, by Montreal's James Wilson Morrice (1865–1924), is a fine work by this most celebrated of Canada's expatriate painters. A close friend of Matisse, he worked principally in Europe and North Africa.

Tom Thomson, the Group of Seven and Emily Carr all have major works here. But of the moderns, by far the most significant represented is Paul-Emile Borduas (1905–60). His *Les signes s'envolent* and *L'étoile noire* are stark, disturbing abstracts by a man who began his career as a painter of church murals and stained glass. Rebelling against conservative religion under the dual influences of surrealism and psychoanalysis, Borduas led the school of Quebec *Automatistes*. They include here outstanding works by Jean-Paul Riopelle, born in 1923.

The best avant-garde art shows in Montreal are held at the **Saidye Bronfman Centre** (5170 Côte-Ste-Catherine).

The small but tastefully de-signed **McCord Museum** (690 Sherbrooke Street West) provides some fascinating insights into Canadian life—Inuit and Indian as well as the world of the fur trader and other pioneers of the 18th and 19th centuries. Dominated by a totem pole from British Columbia, the exhibits include costumes, artefacts, paintings, drawings and magnificent old photographs from the William Notman archives (said to contain over 700,000 prints).

The **Museum of Decorative Arts** *(Musée des arts décoratifs)* is housed in the 20th-century Château Dufresne (corner of Sherbrooke and Boulevard Pie-IX). More palazzo than château with its frescoes and reinforced concrete columns clad in Italian marble, the museum is devoted principally to international modern design in furniture, ceramics, glass and textiles from 1940 to the present day.

Train enthusiasts should head out to the **Canadian Railway Museum** in the southern suburb of St-Constant, 122A Rue St-Pierre. Ride an old tram to the country station where the sheds display historic train engines of the Canadian Pacific and the luxury private coach of William Van Horne, the man who masterminded the building of C.P.R.'s transcontinental railway. On Sundays, you can take a ride in one of the old trains.

EASTERN TOWNSHIPS

Stretching to the border with the states of Vermont and New Hampshire, U.S.A, this pleasant region of farmland and orchards was settled at the end of the 18th century by Loyalist refugees from the American Revolution. There's a distinctly New England flavour to the architecture of white clapboard houses in a landscape of rolling hills, green meadows and lakes rarely bigger than ponds, but the population is today overwhelmingly French-speaking. You may still hear the region referred to by some Québécois as *Cantons de l'Est*, but the newer translation *L'Estrie* is in much more common usage.

East on Motorway 10, a tour of the region makes an easy day trip out of Montreal, but you may well choose to stay longer for a restful boat cruise, picnic or ramble, taking advantage of the many delightful old-fashioned country inns and restaurants using the excellent local farm produce.

Popular with the sailing and windsurfing fraternity, **Lake Brome** and the sleepy country town of **Knowlton** make a pleasant first stop. To see what the farmers are up to, head over on Saturday mornings to the market in **Sutton**.

Take a leisurely boat cruise on **Lake Memphremagog** ("Beautiful Waters"), the region's largest, stretching across the border into Vermont. At **St-Benoît-du-Lac**, look out for the graceful neo-Gothic grey-stone silhouette of the Benedictine abbey, much appreciated for the monks' Gregorian chant. The monks also make and sell some fine cheeses —an Italian-style ricotta, blue Ermite and the Mont St-Benoît, great with the apples they grow in their orchard.

Further east, you'll find the most characteristic New England atmosphere around **Lake Massawippi**, particularly in **North Hatley**, where 19th-century colonial mansions have been converted into elegant inns. The town has some good antique shops. In summer, The Piggery barn provides a home for one of the region's last surviving English-language theatres. Thanks to its situation in a sheltered valley, North Hatley enjoys a particularly pleasant microclimate which attracts hummingbirds and flora of more southern climes.

Over at **Coaticook,** hikers and picnickers tend to head for the wooded ravines along the Coaticook River. In August, the town stages a milk festival with the cows (and some of the milkmaids) dressed in fancy summer bonnets. The great attraction at **Cookshire** is the fragrant June bread festival.

THE LAURENTIANS

The densely forested, rolling mountain range that the Québécois call *les Laurentides* constitutes a favourite summer and winter playground for the people of Montreal. Swimming, sailing, canoeing, waterskiing, fishing, hiking, horse-riding, golf—the list of summer pleasures is endless. In winter, the skating and skiing, downhill and cross-country, are the best in eastern Canada. And the landscape is a pure joy, with long, narrow glacial lakes fed by cold streams gurgling down the granite mountain slopes of yellow birch, beech, sugar maple and fir.

The virgin forests were long a refuge for Algonquin Indians fleeing the Iroquois. The Québécois began to settle there in any great numbers only in the second half of the 19th century, when an enterprising curate, Antoine Labelle of St-Jérôme, promoted it as an alternative for peasants who were otherwise emigrating to New England. This southeastern edge of the great Canadian Shield proved poor farm country and difficult to exploit for logging, but it really came into its own in the 20th century with the development of tourism. In addition to local Montrealers, it attracts steady traffic from New England.

The heart of the resort area is within an easy 90-minute to 2-hour drive of the city for a week-end or longer stay. Motorway 15 north-west from Montreal, then Highway 117 take you into forested foothills immediately beyond the metropolis.

Just 70 km from the city, **St-Sauveur-des-Monts** makes a charming spot to stop for lunch on one of the roadside flowered terraces. In winter, the resort is popular for its floodlit night-skiing. **Ste-Adèle** on the shores of Lac Rond is a favourite with painters and their groupies. The town's **Village de Séraphin** recaptures the atmosphere of life in the Laurentians in the 1880s.

Probably the liveliest resort in the area is **Ste-Agathe-des-Monts**. It boasts plenty of good restaurants and folksong bars *(boîtes à chansons)*, and a famous summer theatre, Le Patriote. Night owls overcome their hangover with a stroll or boat cruise around the Lac des Sables.

The full natural beauty of the Laurentians is best appreciated in **Mont-Tremblant Provincial Park**. Rent a canoe or kayak to explore some of the 500 lakes and rivers that sparkle across an area of 1,500 sq. km. It was the rush of those streams that inspired the Algonquin name *Manitonga Sontana*, Mountain of the Trembling Spirit, emitting its muffled boom when man disturbed its peace. Mont-Tremblant's 2,131-ft Johannsen peak is the highest in the Laurentians. At the **St-Donat** reception centre or other entry points to the park, you'll find detailed maps of self-guiding nature trails with signposts describing the forest's flora and fauna. The park also provides forest guides for group tours. The park's wildlife, even more abundant in the **Rouge-Matawin Nature Reserve** to the north, includes moose, deer, black bear, otter, mink, muskrat, fox and the beloved beaver. Birdwatchers may spot grouse, loon, heron, finches and warblers, while anglers can hope to catch speckled and lake trout, pike, bass and walleye.

Walking off the after-effects of a night on the town in Ste-Agathe.

QUEBEC CITY

Whereas Montreal has become increasingly "Americanized", the provincial capital remains unmistakably, even defiantly Québécois, if not downright "French". It's difficult to miss the point, in this proud cradle of New France, that the town is borrowing a leaf from the book of the modern French republic by calling its provincial parliament the *Assemblée Nationale.* Only 5 per cent of the population do not speak French as their mother tongue.

The historic centre of the city has something of the atmosphere of France's Atlantic port towns in the neighbourhood down by the St. Lawrence River, while the streets and squares up on the promontory offer North Americans a first hint of Paris's Latin Quarter or even Montmartre. Certainly it's a town for that most Parisian of creatures, the *flâneur* or stroller, wandering at leisure through narrow back streets, paying due homage to the monuments of Quebec City's past triumphs and tribulations, but even more alert to the colours and smells of the present.

If Quebec is said to be derived from an Algonquin word meaning "where the river narrows", this becomes most apparent when you see the city's great outcrop of rock, jutting out over the St. Lawrence. It was named Cap Diamant, after the shiny stones that Jacques Cartier mistook for diamonds (see p. 17). Thus, the city dominated river traffic and prospered from a flourishing trade in fur, lumber, shipbuilding, tanneries, furniture and textiles. Modern shipping and the advent of the railways crippled its port activities, and the city now lives from the service industries of tourism and

107

provincial government administration.

For the best view of the city's spectacular location, cross over to the St. Lawrence River's south bank and take the ferry *(traversier)* from the suburb of Lévis. Otherwise head through the airy but unexceptional modern city to the historic centre of Old Quebec, where the fortified Upper and Lower Town stand at the top and bottom of Cap Diamant, linked by a steep road and funicular railway. Apart from the Citadel and Battlefields Park, every sight worth seeing is within easy walking distance, though you may like to try a 45-minute ride in a horse-drawn *calèche* (from the Parc de l'Esplanade).

Upper Town

Start on top of the rock, where the city's principal landmark is a hotel, the **Château Frontenac**, looming over the town since 1893 like the protective fortress it no longer needs. Because of its dramatic location and the fairytale turrets of its Gothic-Renaissance architecture, the C.P.R.'s Frontenac is one of the most charmingly bombastic of all the many grand hotels that the Canadian Pacific and Canadian National railways put up across the country as symbols of their commercial power. It is named after Count Louis de Frontenac, a rascally 17th-century French governor who upset the clergy by encouraging the sale of brandy to the Indians. Take a look inside at the stucco carvings, tapestries and handsome wood panelling.

Behind the hotel, beyond an 1898 statue of Samuel de Champlain, the city's founder, **Dufferin Terrace** offers a magnificent view over the St. Lawrence and downriver to the Ile d'Or-

léans. Stroll alongside a pleasant little garden, **Parc des Gouverneurs**, with its obelisk paying tribute to Generals Wolfe and Montcalm, both killed at the great battle for Quebec in 1759. The terrace is prolonged by the **Promenade des Gouverneurs**,

Château Frontenac—justly regarded as a summit of railway-Renaissance architecture.

continuing the walk along the foot of the citadel towards Battlefields Park.

North of the Frontenac, **Place d'Armes** is the centre of Old Quebec, where troops were mustered and paraded, proclamations read out, criminals whipped or executed. In the middle, the Monument of Faith *(Monument de la Foi)* commemorates the work of French

Catholic missionaries in North America. On the north side of the square, the **Musée du Fort**, 10 Rue Ste-Anne, stages a sound and light show alternately in English and French on the military history of Quebec City.

Artists gather in the narrow **Rue du Trésor** at the north-west corner of the Place d'Armes to display their works or paint your portrait. The street leads into the city's "**Latin Quarter**", with a quite Parisian air to the 18th-century houses, cafés and bookshops around Rue Couillard, Rue St-Flavien and Rue Hébert.

The neighbourhood's "Latin" derives from the scholarship of a **Seminary**, Rue de l'Université, founded in 1663 by the first bishop of Quebec, François de Montmorency Laval. In the summer, open-air concerts are held in the courtyard. In the **Musée de l'Amérique française,** you will find a detailed history of North American Francophones and an impressive collection of artefacts acquired by priests during their travels in the 19th century.

Set back behind tall trees off the Rue des Jardins, the Anglican **Holy Trinity Cathedral** of 1804, with its elegant spire, will be familiar to Londoners for its respectful imitation of St. Martin-in-the-Fields. It was the first Anglican cathedral to be built outside the British Isles. Notice its solid old pews of English oak.

In an attractive garden setting, the large **Ursuline Convent** was established in 1639 and rebuilt twice after fire. Its **chapel** has a fine 18th-century altar painting and pulpit. Montcalm's skull and humerus are buried in the crypt. One room of the **museum** is devoted to the convent's first mother superior who compiled the first dictionary of the Iroquois and Algonquin languages. The pasture for the convent's cattle is now the quiet, spacious **Parc de l'Esplanade,** the perfect place to rest your tired sightseeing feet.

Lower Town

Various stairways and the winding Côte de la Montagne take you down past Montmorency Park to the site of Champlain's original colony which grew into the **Ville Basse** (Lower Town). One of the more hazardous ways down, and so a favourite with children, is the **Escalier Casse-Cou** (Breakneck Stairway), merely dangerous when wet, lethal when icy. For the view, take the **funicular railway** from Dufferin Terrace. The funicular's Lower Town terminal was once the house of Louis Joliet, great 17th-century fur trader and explorer of the Mississippi River.

Champlain's *Abitation* of 1608 —two wooden houses and a storehouse for furs surrounded by a stockade and a ditch—stood on the **Place Royale**, now a 🏃

beautifully restored square of elegant 17th- and 18th-century houses. In the centre is a replica of a 1686 bust of Louis XIV. Facing the Place Royale, the church of **Notre-Dame-des-Victoires** celebrates French victories over the British *before* 1759.

After centuries of devastation by war, fire, plunder and sheer neglect, the meticulous restoration work by the Quebec provincial government has been a major act of faith in the cultural legacy of New France, reinforcing the provincial motto *Je me souviens*. After 1759, most colonial administrators and merchants just abandoned Quebec, while many who stayed on moved to the shelter of the new British defences in the Upper Town. During the 19th and early 20th centuries, older buildings were often arbitrarily razed to make way for waterfront warehouses and workshops.

Among the historic houses on Rue du Marché-Champlain, **Maison Chevalier** (1752) has become a museum of old Québécois furniture and domestic utensils. The Maison Dumont (1689) on Place Royale is now the **Maison des Vins**, selling good *French* wine and owned, like all Québécois wine and alcohol retailers, by the provincial government. On the corner of the Ruelle du Porche, **Maison Milot** (1691) is notable for its splendidly sturdy roof beams.

(It is currently closed to the public.)

The quaintest of the city's **antique shops** have clustered around Rue Sault-au-Matelot and Rue St-Paul down by the port.

The city has renovated the warehouses of the **Old Port** *(Vieux Port)* as an entertainment area with concerts, open-air theatre, a craftware market, fresh farm produce and a couple of handsome old sailing ships.

Beyond the City Wall

From the Parc de l'Esplanade, drive up the Côte de la Citadelle hill road and through a tunnel for a guided tour around a powerful bastion of fears long gone. The French built the star-shaped **Citadel** between 1690 and 1713 to resist the British. The British enlarged it from 1747 to defend Quebec City against the Americans, but their cannons never fired a shot. The garrison was British-manned for only 20 years before being handed over to Canadian troops. Today it is the home of Canada's crack Royal 22nd Regiment.

The garrison comes to life in the summer with the **Changing of the Guard** (10 a.m. daily) and **Beating the Retreat** (6 p.m. Tuesday, Thursday, Saturday and Sunday). The old powder house serves now as the **22nd Regiment Museum,** displaying an impres-

111

sive range of trophies, weapons and uniforms.

Running south-west from the Parc de l'Esplanade, the broad, modern Grande-Allée runs past the **Assemblée Nationale** (provincial parliament) built from 1877–1886 in the favoured style of the time, French Renaissance. This has been the citadel of Quebec's quest for a special identity in or outside the Canadian Confederation, especially under prime minister René Lévesque.

On Boulevard René Lévesque, the **Grand Théâtre** was inaugurated in 1971 as Quebec City's arts centre and home of the Quebec Symphony Orchestra.

Battlefields Park *(Parc des Champs de Bataille)* is devoted to the momentous battle on the Plains of Abraham that decided the fate of Quebec in 1759. Quite apart from its historical

significance, the park offers fine walks across tree-lined fields.

In the centre of the park you'll see one of the three massive **Martello towers** built between 1808 and 1811. Believed impregnable against the artillery of that era, they were to defend Quebec from a potential American attack. The towers have exhibitions in the summer. In a town where every monument seems like a political statement, Rue Wolfe leads to

Place Royale is a little more appropriately French in feeling than the Changing of the Guard.

one on the spot where General Wolfe was mortally wounded, while anonymous Québécois patriots have responded with a statue of Joan of Arc, off the Avenue George VI.

In the southern half of the park, the **Musée du Québec** pos-

The catch is in, and the fishermen have all gone home at Rocher Percé on the Gaspé Peninsula.

sesses a first-rate collection of Québécois painting and sculpture. The paintings date from the colony's beginnings to the present day; the epoch of the sculpture on show varies with each exhibition. Look out for the historical studies of Joseph Légaré, the portraits of Antoine Plamondon and Théodore Hamel and landscapes of Cornelius Krieghoff. Among the moderns are the *Automatiste* abstracts of Jean-Paul Riopelle and the optical art of Jacques Hurtubise.

COTE DE CHARLEVOIX

A day trip along the St. Lawrence River on Highway 360 north of Quebec City will give you a glimpse of village life and the challenging landscape in which the *habitants* created their farms. Côte de Charlevoix is part of the Laurentian heights, reaching to the Saguenay River where the *coureurs de bois* turned off in search of furs.

At the northern edge of town, turn right after the Montmorency River bridge into a park where a terrace overlooks the impressive **Montmorency Falls** plunging 274 ft into the river.

Ste-Anne-de-Beaupré is a major pilgrimage town for torch-lit

where you can buy handmade paper, perfect for writing home with distinction. On the wharf, take a ferry across to the lovely little **Ile aux Coudres**, another fishing community that has become a favourite artists' haunt. The island's homecrafts include weaving the rough Québécois rag rugs known as *catalognes*. You may be tempted into an overnight stay by the colourful inns and folksong taverns run by retired seamen, who look as if they escaped the old schooner stranded at the south-west end of the island. These salts do cook up a fine heart-warming fish soup. When Jacques Cartier got to the island, his sailors made a feast of the hazelnuts, for which *coudres* is an old French word.

Ever since U.S. president William H. Taft built himself a holiday home out at Pointe-au-Pic at the beginning of the century, **La Malbaie** has enjoyed a reputation as the region's smartest resort town, offering horse-riding, golf and tennis. Stop at the grand old **Manoir Richelieu** hotel at least for tea on the superbly manicured lawns overlooking the river.

processions in summer to the glory of the mother of the Virgin Mary. Beyond the town, in a sudden confrontation with the wilderness, a walkway in the forest takes you up close to the pounding waters of the 240-ft **Ste-Anne Falls**, ragged and crashing around the boulders, a much less neat and tidy cascade than Montmorency.

Painters and craftsmen have made their home in the fishing village of **Baie-St-Paul** and will be more than happy to sell you their work.

In a country boasting one of the world's biggest paper industries, you'll find here one last town, **St-Joseph-de-la-Rive**,

GASPE PENINSULA

Gaspé, the first Canadian landfall of Jacques Cartier in 1534, is a Micmac Indian word for Land's End, and this is indeed southern Quebec's remotest region, 700 km from Quebec City. But it's well worth the trip for anyone with four or five days to spare and seeking to get away from the throng into this still unspoiled wilderness on the Gulf of St. Lawrence.

Densely wooded river valleys and sheltered coves break up the rugged north coast, with its steep cliffs plunging down to broad pebble or fine sandy beaches. The Chics-Chocs Mountains of the interior, the highest in eastern Canada, are the northern "terminal" of the Appalachian Range that begins down in Alabama.

Descendants of Acadians and Loyalists, the warm and friendly Gaspesians are a more harmonious mix of French- and English-speaking citizens than elsewhere in Quebec. In a region without any noteworthy industry other than cod fishing, a little forestry and tourism, the people add to their income by selling their craftwork and farm produce from improvised stands. This is where to get your picnic supplies (fruit, vegetables, fish, honey and doughnuts) but also nicely handmade sweaters for chilly evenings.

At the tip of the peninsula, **Forillon National Park** offers great facilities for fishing, boat cruises, skin-diving (rubber suits are obligatory) and hiking. In this most spectacular of land-

and seascapes, even the least artistic of you will be tempted to take up painting or at least photography. Look out for the whales and grey seals in the gulf. The whales usually announce their presence by very audible heavy breathing when they surface. Wildlife inside the park includes fat little porcupine, hare, red squirrel, deer, moose and an occasional bear, lynx and fox. Birdwatchers have 200 species to feast their eyes on, with guillemots and cormorants among the easier to spot.

The town of **Gaspé** makes its livelihood from fishing—cod and herring. It offers good opportunities for sailing and windsurfing (again, rubber suits obligatory). On the Rue du Monument is a **granite cross**, commemorating the wooden cross that Jacques Cartier planted on behalf of his French sovereign in front of a bemused audience of Iroquois.

The best hotels are in the resort town of **Percé**, and so this is naturally the most crowded place on the peninsula. People come for watersports and to marvel at the cliffs pierced *(percé)* by the sea. The erosion originally created two arches in the 282-ft-high rocks, but one has since crumbled. See them at sunrise when they're pink. Take a cruise around **Bonaventure Island** to view the gannets and penguins.

THE ATLANTIC

The Atlantic coastal provinces lie off Canada's beaten track. This implies many advantages for tourists seeking lovely unspoiled countryside away from the crowds, but also, for the residents, some acute political and economic disadvantages. Nova Scotia, Prince Edward Island (P.E.I.) and New Brunswick make up the Maritime Provinces, more commonly known as the Maritimes. Last to join the Canadian Confederation, in 1949, the offshore island of Newfoundland is linked as one province with the mainland region of Labrador.

The Maritimes and Newfoundland have often felt neglected. They were the last provinces to benefit from transcontinental railways and highways. New Brunswick's shipbuilding timber suffered in the age of steam and steel hulls. Newfoundland's fisheries were equally hard

hit when modern refrigeration made it possible for foreign companies to dispense with the island's centuries-old drying techniques. Economic hardship prompted some to migrate to other regions.

But their separateness has shaped a hardy people of considerable character and charm. Just getting to know them makes the journey worthwhile. You'll find them cheerful, friendly and more easily approachable than the big city folk of Ontario and Quebec. Newfoundland is peopled almost exclusively from the south-west of England and southern Ireland, whence the special music and colour of their dialect (see p. 142). The Maritimes have been mainly settled by Scottish Highlanders, German Protestants and French-speaking Acadians.

The cooler climate makes the region a strictly summer and early autumn destination. It's a land of hiking, camping and fishing, with some good swimming off Prince Edward Island and Nova Scotia. If the Maritimes are warm to mellow from late June to early September, Newfoundland is a little fresher.

NOVA SCOTIA

You'd think the chamber of commerce carved their map as a public relations gimmick, but the province really is shaped like a lobster. In any case, many a gourmet or glutton feels that a Halifax lobster dinner is reason enough to make the trip. But weight watchers can enjoy Nova Scotia, too.

There's the sparkling Atlantic coastline, with its delightful little fishing ports. Or rolling green hills across the interior to the orchards and dairy farms of Annapolis Valley. This western side of the peninsula is rich in the poignant history of French Acadia. The province's northern island is the site of one of Canada's best-loved national parks, Cape Breton Highlands, where you'll drive the spectacular Cabot Trail along the coast and in and out of the forest.

Halifax

Ships of the Canadian navy jostle with the trawlers of Nova Scotia's commercial fisheries in this major Atlantic port. But the prevailing tone is one of more relaxed pleasure, typified by the yachts and sailboats gliding gracefully in and out of the Northwest Arm marinas.

Attracted by the natural harbour, one of the world's largest, the British established the town in the mid-18th century as a naval garrison and shipyard to

Even a late bird gets something from the pickings down at Peggy's Cove.

118

counter the French fortress of Louisbourg further north on Cape Breton (see p. 128). Halifax's strategic position on the Atlantic soon proved even more invaluable as a base for "farming" the rich shoals of cod and herring on the ocean's Scotian Shelf. In this haven for pirates and rum-runners, Samuel Cunard (1787–1865) founded his famous transatlantic shipping line with a fortune acquired in large part from privateering.

Down on the harbourfront today, the old wharves, warehouses—even the houses of joyous ill-repute that cluster in back streets around any international port—have been refurbished as **Historic Properties**, a bright and breezy neighbourhood of artists' studios and galleries, shops, restaurants and taverns with open-air terraces. The boardwalk takes you through a colourful architecture of red brick, timber, grey stone and gaily painted clapboard. Summer attractions include concerts, lobster races and wind-surfing competitions. The international competition of town criers no longer takes place here, but you might hear the official city town crier in traditional costume, who is in the area throughout the summer season.

Anchored by Privateers' Warehouse (Halifax was a popular haven for pirates from the Napoleonic Wars to the rum-

running Prohibition Era of the 1920s) is a grand racing schooner, **Bluenose II**. You can walk the decks or even take a 2-hour cruise on this replica of the famous 1921 champion sailship portrayed on the Canadian ten-cent coin. "Bluenose" was the Americans' nickname for Nova Scotia's wind-whipped sailors. If the schooner is out of port on one of its frequent goodwill tours down the Atlantic

In Halifax Harbour, the wind is up and the surfing's easy.

coast, there are several other **harbour cruises** well worth taking, to view the shipyards, naval installations and fishing fleet, as well as the yacht clubs and elegant waterfront homes on the Northwest Arm inlet.

Also on the harbour, the **Maritime Museum of the Atlantic** (Lower Water Street) is housed in a turn-of-the-century ship chandlery, setting the tone with a nostalgic whiff of tarred rope in the restored shop on the ground floor. The museum traces the dockyards' 200-year history, displaying naval instruments, weapons, and some superb ship models from sail to steam, including the *Aquitania* ocean liner. A special section is devoted

121

to shipwrecks and lifesaving. Berthed at the museum's wharf is the 1913 survey vessel, *Acadia,* that charted the coasts of eastern Canada from Nova Scotia to Hudson Bay.

Downtown, on Hollis Street, **Province House** is a dignified Georgian stone building (1818) boasting Canada's oldest legislative assembly, instigated by New England Loyalists. A **statue** of Joseph Howe stands in front; he was Nova Scotia's champion of a free press and democratic government, but a fierce opponent of joining the Confederation.

For a good panoramic view of Halifax and a sense of its important military history, make your way around the grassy slopes leading to the star-shaped **Citadel**, from which a cannon-shot has boomed across the town each day at noon since the 1850s. A good guided tour takes you around the garrison, originally built for 300 British soldiers. It is surrounded by a deep, wide dry moat, thick walls and fortified grass-covered earthworks. The Cavalier Building has been restored to the way it was in 1869 and is now an **Army Museum**, with uniforms, weapons and the models of three previous city fortresses. The South Magazine stored powder barrels uncomfortably close to military prisoners who were kept, with the cannons, in the Garrison Cells.

Canadian troops used the Citadel as barracks in both world wars, while anti-aircraft batteries were installed there in World War II. In summer, students in the kilted uniform of the 78th Highlanders perform infantry and artillery drills. The **Nova Scotia Tattoo** stages more spectacular military bagpipe parades, highland dances, singing and a Naval Gun Run competition at the nearby Halifax Metro Centre in late June or early July, depending on the year.

From the Citadel, looking east, you can see the city's popular landmark, the **Old Town Clock**. This octagonal tower was erected in 1803 by Prince Edward, tough commander of the Nova Scotia forces and future father of Queen Victoria. At the south end of Grand Parade, opposite the city hall, stands **St. Paul's** (1750), Canada's oldest Anglican church.

West of the Citadel, on Summer Street, the **Nova Scotia Museum** is devoted to the province's human and natural history. Its exhibits include Indian clothing, tools and artefacts and there is a separate section on the people of Arcadia. Amongst the regional wildlife on display, you can see dinosaurs, moose, bears, coyotes and bald eagles as well as a range of other mammals, birds and marine animals.

The **Public Gardens** south of

the museum makes a pleasant stroll around the duck pond and among such exquisite oriental trees as the Chinese gingko and white-flowered dove tree, the Japanese lilac and larch, and a corkscrew birch. Try to be there for an utterly Victorian open-air band concert.

The town's most attractive piece of greenery is **Point Pleasant Park**, whose beach and shady woods make it ideal for picnics. At the southern tip of the Halifax peninsula, the park provides a fine vantage point from which to watch the big ships in the harbour and the yachts on the Northwest Arm. Among old ruined fortifications is the still intact **Prince of Wales Martello Tower**, a massive stone structure serving as barracks, weapons storage and artillery platform, built by Prince Edward in 1796.

Collectors of lore about the *Titanic* ocean liner, which sank south of Newfoundland in 1912, can find the tombs of many of the victims in the **Fairview Cemetery** on the north-west side of town.

Atlantic Coast

Scores of lighthouses along Nova Scotia's south shore trace a saw-toothed route of coves that over the ages offered shelter to pirates, rum-runners and fishermen. For the modern holiday-maker, there are plenty of pleasant bathing beaches, too.

The 45-minute drive along winding coastal Highway 333 from Halifax south-west to **Peggy's Cove** has become a photographer's pilgrimage. This almost unbearably picturesque fishing village perches its brightly coloured clapboard cottages and lighthouse among massive granite boulders. The trick is to keep the snack-bars and souvenir shops out of the picture.

You'll find more deserted coves and beaches around St. Margaret's Bay as you drive on west to **Chester** on Mahone Bay. This fashionable resort town was founded in 1759 by Massachusetts fishermen and remains a favourite vacation spot for New Englanders.

Inland, 20 minutes' drive from Chester north along Highway 12, you can visit **Ross Farm**, a living museum of 300 years of Nova Scotia farming. Oxcarts and horse-drawn haywagons take you around the property, where you can watch barrel-making, see the old farm implements in action, buy produce from the farm kitchen and locally made craftware.

Take a boat trip from the town of Mahone Bay to **Oak Island**. Dreamers still dig for the gold doubloons, emeralds, rubies and diamonds that Captain William Kidd, lovable villain of Robert

123

Louis Stevenson's *Treasure Island*, is said to have buried there. This real-life Scots-born 17th-century brigand received the official blessing of the British governor of New York to plunder French, Spanish and Dutch ships from the Caribbean to Madagascar, frequently hiding out on the Nova Scotia coast. That blessing didn't keep him from being hanged in London, convicted of murder and acts of piracy.

Down the coast from Mahone Bay, **Lunenburg**, the original 18th-century settlement of German Protestants, is an attractive town of grey-weathered shingle-board houses. Its proud boast in modern times is the building of the original *Bluenose* racing schooner. On the waterfront, the **Fisheries Museum of the Atlantic** will give you a vivid sense of the whole history of sailing and fishing along Nova Scotia's coasts. Besides a beautiful model of the *Bluenose*, the museum's star attractions are two old ships moored in the port: the *Theresa E. Connor* schooner used for cod fishing and the *Cape Sable* trawler.

Across Lunenburg Harbour,

take a clifftop hike through the little pine forest and around the striking rock formations of **The Ovens**. These deep caves were the scene of a mini gold rush in 1861, when New Englanders poured into the area to pan a few, very few nuggets from the shale on the beach. A little museum shows you their tools, techniques and a few molar-sized bits of gold.

The bitter events of deportation are all but forgotten at apple-blossom time in Acadia's Annapolis Valley.

Annapolis Valley

Route 101 takes you from Halifax north-west across the peninsula through Annapolis Valley's fertile farmland of apple orchards, strawberry fields and cattle pastures. This is the heart of Nova Scotia's French Acadia.

In Windsor, stop off to see the 18th-century blockhouse at **Fort Edward** (named after Governor Edward Cornwallis), grim monument to the British military presence that prepared the deportation.

The dispersal began out at **Grand-Pré,** now a national historic park commemorating the Acadians' resilience. This was the centre of a thriving farming community which built dykes to reclaim marshland from the Minas Basin, grow fruit and vegetables and raise cattle, sheep,

pigs and poultry. Their farms were destroyed by the British in 1704, recaptured by the French in 1747 and held just eight years till the 2,000-strong community was expelled, to return a few years later and re-establish their farms all over again. A stone church, faintly Norman in style, was erected in the park in 1930 as a memorial to Acadian culture and history. The bronze statue in the gardens is not a saint, but Evangeline, sad heroine of Henry Longfellow's poem on the deportation.

Along the Annapolis River road, such pretty little villages as **Middleton, Lawrencetown** and **Bridgetown** bear the unmistakable mark of the New Englanders who moved into the region to take over the Acadians' farms.

On the estuary, the peaceful town of **Annapolis Royal** was once the beleaguered target of 14 British and French sieges and countless pirate raids. Formerly Port Royal, it was renamed after England's Queen Anne and became capital of Nova Scotia until the foundation of Halifax. **Fort Anne**, focus for the belligerence, is now a pleasant park of grassy knolls and ridges, remains of the earthwork defences. Of the original buildings, only a powder house in the south-west bastion and a storehouse in the north-west survive. The officers quart-

ers of 1797 have been reconstructed to house a **museum** of local Indian culture and natural history.

Epitome of the town's more peaceful side, the **Historic Gardens** south of the city centre display flora representative of the region's inhabitants: iris and the vegetables the Acadians grew, with a reconstruction of their ingenious system of dykes and a typical Acadian cottage; an English rose garden with a collection of over 2,000 bushes and Victorian flower beds. A **marsh lookout** gives you a good view over the estuary.

In the town centre, the shops and taverns on **Lower St. George Street** are being transformed to recapture the grace of the town's Victorian era.

Port Royal (10 km west along Highway 1) is a fine recreation of Samuel de Champlain's sturdy timbered *Habitation*, built in 1605. Furniture, utensils and craftware, supplemented by audiovisual shows, give a vivid insight into the earliest permanent European settlement north of Florida. You can see how the first French settlers, just 60 to begin with, made friendly contact with Micmac Indians. And hear how Champlain kept up morale throughout the long winters with a social club, *L'Ordre du Bon Temps* (The Order of Good Times). Each member would organize a fortnightly banquet of game and fish he had caught himself. Among the entertainments they concocted to cheer up the long cold evenings was a play, *Le Théâtre de Neptune*. North America's first known full-length drama was written by the colony's lawyer, Marc Lescarbot. His writings, along with Champlain's journals, provided the basis for the meticulous reconstitution of their environment.

Bitter-Sweet Acadia

Before the British came, the region of the Maritimes was known as Acadia, a corruption of Arcadia, the Ancient Greeks' "Peaceful Land" which 16th-century explorer Verrazzano imagined transported to the New World. Indeed, after the initial shock of rigorous winters on the Bay of Fundy, the first French colonists (under Henri IV in the 1600s) settled down to farm the rich soil and fish the waters in harmony with their Micmac Indian neighbours.

But trouble began in 1621, when Edinburgh-born James I of England authorized a charter to settle the land as New Scotland—Nova Scotia. Living far from the fur traders of Quebec, the defenceless Acadians found their land had become a bargaining counter in the Anglo-French power struggle. This strategic link between New France and New England was swapped back and forth until the 1713 Treaty of Utrecht finally handed over to the British all of Acadia except Cape Breton Island (lost after Louisbourg's capture in 1758).

From 2,000 in 1713, the Aca-dians had multiplied to a prosperous community of 12,000 by 1755, regarded by the British as a danger to security. They claimed to be neutral, refusing to swear allegiance to the Crown as they knew it would enforce military service against the French. Charles Lawrence, lieutenant governor of Nova Scotia, organized deportation of some 10,000 men, women and children, often splitting up families and scattering them around North America. Some ended up as far away as Louisiana, where their descendants are known as Cajuns. With uncharacteristic French understatement, the upheaval was known as le Grand Dérangement *(the Great Disturbance).*

Many returned a few years later, after defeat in Quebec ended the French threat in North America. Finding their lands had been given to American Loyalist settlers, the Acadians set about building a new life. Today, they number close to 500,000, with the largest community in New Brunswick, where a centre of Acadian studies at the University of Moncton sustains an awareness of the proud old culture.

127

Cape Breton Island

The airport outside the steel town of Sydney is the most convenient gateway for both the Fortress of Louisbourg National Historic Park to the east and the Cabot Trail to the west leading to Cape Breton Highlands National Park.

You may like to drive the more roundabout coast road over to Louisbourg with a side trip to **Glace Bay**. As an intriguing exercise in modern industrial archaeology, its desolate log cabins and colliery installations have become a coal mining village **museum**. Take the fascinating trip along the shafts and galleries of the abandoned Ocean Deep Mine which reaches 17 km under the sea. You can have a coal miner's meal at the colliery canteen.

The great French fortress town of **Louisbourg** is presented as a splendid national historic park, one of the most elaborate in Canada's ambitious reconstruction programme. You'll need a full day to do it justice. After the guided tour, take time to discuss extra details of 18th-century French colonial life with the well-informed and entertaining costumed volunteers performing the roles of fishermen, merchants, soldiers and craftsmen.

Building of the original fortress began in 1719, six years after the Treaty of Utrecht had left the French only Cape Breton Island. The ice-free port provided a year-round strategic defence of approaches to the Gulf of St. Lawrence and Quebec, and a commercial base for cod fishing, trade with the Caribbean and smuggling to and from New England. The reconstruction of a quarter of the town recaptures life as it was in the summer of 1744, a year before the first great British siege, 16 years before it was destroyed.

You are plunged into the atmosphere of that "moment in time" as soon as you get off the park bus at the Georges des Roches fishing property, a long turf-roofed log cabin outside the fortified town. The men may be laying out dozens of cod to dry on flakes—the same trestled wooden racks still in use in fishing villages all down the coast. At the drawbridge to **Porte Dauphine**, the main entrance gate bearing a relief of three fleurs-de-lys, the French royal coat of arms, you'll be stopped by French soldiers to check whether you're not a British spy.

If they let you through (they usually do), walk past the Dauphin bastion to the handsomely carved stone portside gate, **Porte Frédéric**. Turn right into the town along the main street, past the hospitable eating establishments of the Hôtel de la Marine and L'Epée Royale, where you can get a characteristic 18th-century meal served on tin or pewter plates. Continue over to the **King's Bastion**, the military barracks where living conditions show the kind of stark contrast that nurtured enough discontent to cause a mutiny in that year of 1744. The gabled Governor's Wing numbers ten luxurious apartments with fine furniture, tapestries, silks, brocades, silverware and delicate porcelain. The neighbouring Officers' Quarters are more humble but still comfortable enough, while the ordinary soldiers' barracks are downright miserable with rudimentary beds of straw. In the middle of the block, a simple little chapel tries to keep the peace.

Back in Sydney, follow the Trans-Canada Highway west to the Englishtown exit for the ferry across St. Ann's Bay to join the **Cabot Trail** at Indian Brook. This 300-km trail offers one of the country's most spectacular drives, with dramatic juxtapositions of dense pine forest, sheer cliffs and the ocean. Travel north along the **Gaelic Coast**, a name amply justified by the thick Scottish burr you'll hear from most of the very friendly people you speak to on the way. At **Cape Smokey**, so called for the fogs that shroud it in winter and a few unlucky summer days, take the ski-lift which operates in summer for the view up and

down the coast and over to the Cape Breton Highlands.

Ingonish is a popular resort town with fine sandy beaches, offering excellent sailing, fishing and swimming. Take at least a drink at the Keltic Lodge hotel, an old Nova Scotia landmark worth a visit for its view of Cape Smokey.

Cape Breton Highlands National Park is a joy for all naturelovers. The Cabot Trail leads you around the periphery, but clearly marked hiking trails (maps at the Ingonish park entrance) take you into the interior. Among the best are the Glasgow Lakes trail to John Deer Lake and the trail around Beulach Ban Falls and French Mountain. Camping facilities are of course better equipped on the edge than those marked out inside the forest. These "New Scottish" highlands look uncannily like those in the old country. To ram the point home, there's even a Scottish shepherd's cottage, **Lone Shieling**, off the highway at Grande Anse River. The forest, a mixture of conifers and hardwoods, shelters white-tailed deer, black bear, moose, beaver, red fox, lynx, mink and snowshoe hare. Bird-watchers can spot, among many species, redtailed hawk and the occasional bald eagle. Fishermen should get their licence at the park entrance to angle for trout or salmon

(river-bank, wading, rowboat, but no motorboats).

On the north-east corner of the park, **Neil Harbour** is a pleasant little fishing port with sandy beaches.

To explore the northern tip of the island, leave the park at South Harbour and drive 16 km to the fishing village of **Bay St. Lawrence**. Following a common seaport custom, the white clapboard **village church**, with its

During Gaelic summer festivities, Nova Scotians out-Scot the Scots in Picton County.

nave shaped like an upturned ship, was designed and built by local shipwrights. Take a bracing hike along the grassy cliff top west of town, but beware of the winds.

South-west of the park,

Chéticamp is an old stronghold of Acadian culture, with a **museum** exhibiting craftware as it was crocheted, spun, hooked or woven in bygone centuries. At the museum's little restaurant, you can sample a traditional meal of clam chowder, meat pâté and molasses cakes. Expert anglers insist that the salmon fishing near **Margaree Forks** is the best in eastern Canada. North East Margaree has a **salmon museum** devoted to the fish's life cycle and the cunning tricks of poachers.

In a fairytale setting of wooded hills around Bras d'Or (Golden Arm) Lake, **Baddeck** likes to be known as the place in which telephone-inventor Alexander Graham Bell chose to spend the last, very active years of his life. His home, hidden in the forest, is not open to the public, but the superbly organized museum in the **Alexander Graham Bell National Historic Park** shows how the great man devoted his energies in Baddeck to aviation. Besides his invention of the tetrahedral kite, the exhibits illustrate his work on the telephone and inventions of medical and maritime instruments. The museum gives plenty of space to photos of his family life in Edinburgh, the United States and Baddeck—which reminded him of countryside near Edinburgh.

If this has whetted your taste for things Scottish, end your tour at the southern tip of St. Ann's Bay, where **Gaelic College** gives summer courses in bagpipe-playing, dancing and tartan-weaving. Even if you're not tempted to sign up, you can watch classes in progress. In August, the **Gaelic Mod** gathers Scots old and Nova for a grand competition.

PRINCE EDWARD ISLAND

Canada's smallest province, just 240 km long and only 80 km across at its widest point, has a gentle rural atmosphere of rolling green meadows in the interior, with a coast of long sandy beaches at the foot of terracotta cliffs. The island nestles snugly in the Gulf of St. Lawrence, separated from New Brunswick and Nova Scotia by the Northumberland Strait. More than three-quarters of the area is given over to farmland. Rich in iron oxides, the red soil's main crop is potatoes, but farmers also grow succulent blueberries, raspberries and strawberries. If the island's lobsters are a worthy rival to Nova Scotia's, its finest seafood is the oysters of Malpeque Bay.

Jacques Cartier named the island Ile St-Jean when he spotted it in the 16th century, but the French didn't colonize it until after their retrenchment following the 1713 Treaty of Utrecht. Like Nova Scotia, the island was transformed by the Acadians' deportation and their replacement by New Englanders, who named it after Prince Edward, Duke of Kent, in 1799. The New Englanders preferred to exploit their property as absentee landlords, leaving it mainly to Irish and Scottish immigrants to clear the forests for shipbuilding and agriculture. P.E.I.'s great historic moment came in 1864, when its capital, Charlottetown, hosted a meeting of Maritime leaders with delegates from Ontario and Quebec to chart the path to Canada's federal status as a united dominion.

After potatoes (winning P.E.I. the name of "Spud Island", a less grandiloquent alternative to "Cradle of Confederation"), tourism rates as the number two industry. The superb sandy beaches of the north coast attract over half a million visitors a year. Fans of Lucy Maud Montgomery's novel *Anne of Green Gables* can visit here the landscape in which it was set.

After visiting centrally located Charlottetown, you can take three well-signposted scenic drives around the island: Blue Heron in the centre, Lady Slipper to the west and Kings Byway to the east, corresponding roughly to the three counties, Queens, Prince and Kings.

Charlottetown

P.E.I.'s only city sets the tone of the island's low-key charm. Named after the wife of George III of England, the town offers a colourful mix of greenery, characteristic red stone and Victorian gingerbread. It's a busy port, a commercial and tourist centre, but remains resolutely old-fashioned.

Starting in Confederation Plaza, visit **Province House**, the sober grey sandstone Georgian building in which the "Fathers of the Confederation" met in 1864. Originally a courthouse, it is now the seat of the provincial legislature. **Confederation Chamber** has been preserved with the names of the august delegates, a very dignified setting for an affair that was in fact characterized by somewhat extravagant wining and dining.

Next door stands the modern **Confederation Centre of the Arts**, opened in 1964 to commemorate the Confederation Conference's centenary. The complex includes a museum, art gallery, theatre and library. Look in the gallery for the late-19th-century work of P.E.I. portraitist Robert Harris, celebrated for his group picture of the Fathers of the Confederation. The centre is also the focus for the Charlottetown Summer Festival.

Across the street, **Cows Ice Cream** store used to be the oldest operating pharmacy in Canada. Many of the original fittings are still in place.

You'll find exhibits relating to the island's history in **Beaconsfield,** a gracious Victorian mansion on Kent Street. In July, the annual Strawberry Fair takes over the grounds.

Blue Heron Drive

The 180-km circuit follows the north shore, with its barrier islands, windswept dunes, red cliffs and salt marshes, and around to the Northumberland Strait. From Charlottetown, head north to the great sandy beaches of **P.E.I. National Park**. The north shore's amazingly warm water (22°C in summer) offers the balmiest bathing in the Maritimes. The park also includes the most popular attraction on the whole island, **Green Gables House,** a neat white-frame farmhouse with green shutters and roof. Lucy Maud Montgomery lived here as a child and later used it as the setting for her novel.

Lady Slipper Drive

Starting out from Summerside, this 260-km western circuit, named after the provincial flower, takes you through the French-speaking population (approx. 2,500) living on the south coast around Egmont Bay. Many of the villages fly the Acadians'

Anne of Greenbacks
The P.E.I. tourist industry wrings every last drop from the Green Gables saga, written in 1908 with endless sequels. Besides the house, fans can also visit the author's birthplace (New London); the Green Gables Post Office (Cavendish); Anne's "House of Dreams" (French River), a recreation of the fictional home of Anne and her new husband; and Anne of Green Gables Museum at Park Corner. Nostalgics of the Anne Shirley movie of the 1930s can compare it with Charlottetown Summer Festival's annual theatre production of Anne of Green Gables as a musical comedy.

blue, white and red flag modelled on that of France, but with a single star added to the blue band. Visit the **Miscouche Acadian Museum,** just west of Summerside and an Acadian Pioneer Settlement at **Mont-Carmel**. The island's 19th-century shipbuilding industry is featured in **Green Park** museum and historic house at Port Hill. Gourmets head straight for the renowned oysters of Malpeque Bay. Out in the bay, on Lennox Island, is a settlement of Mi'kmaq Indians.

Kings Byway Drive

East of Charlottetown, the longest of the circuits, 384 km, encompasses pleasant beaches,

rugged, red-stone capes and coves, shady forests, lobster and tuna fisheries, and potato and fruit farms.

At the **Orwell Corner Historic Village** experience the 1800s atmosphere of its church, farmhouse, school, shingle mill and smithy. Visit the **Basin Head Fisheries Museum** at the east end of the island. On the north shore, at **Red Head,** boats can be chartered for deep-sea fishing.

NEW BRUNSWICK

With a rugged coastline and an interior covered 80 per cent by forest, the province is popular with nature-loving campers, fishermen and hunters. Anglers can hope for trout, bass, pickerel and salmon, while hunters go for the duck and grouse. Wildlife enthusiasts may also spot white-tailed deer, black bear and moose in the forests. The Bay of Fundy's 48-foot-high tides produce remark-

You'll find that not all the houses on Prince Edward Island are green or even gabled.

had trickled back after their deportation during the Anglo-French wars. Today, one-third of the population is French-speaking, the rest English.

Saint John

The province's largest town (where it is the custom never to abbreviate "Saint" to "St.") is a port in the estuary of the Saint John River. It is the centre of an important paper and pulp industry as well as shipyards and oil refineries, but the city fathers have worked miracles to beautify the waterfront. Mists rising from the Bay of Fundy add a touch of romance and mystery.

One of the town's main attractions is the natural phenomenon of the Bay of Fundy's extraordinary tides, with a variation from low to high tide of 28 ft at the mouth of the Saint John River. Watch the **Reversing Falls Rapids** from the bridge on Highway 100. The tourist information office there will tell you the best times to watch the tides' evolution. At low tide, the Fundy's waters are 14 ft lower than the Saint John River, causing it to cascade through a narrow

able effects in the river estuaries and along the coast.

Linked to Nova Scotia by the narrow Chignecto Isthmus, New Brunswick became a separate province in 1784 at the demand of 14,000 Loyalist refugees. It took its name from the German duchy then ruled by George III of England. The Loyalists joined earlier settlers from New England, Pennsylvania and Yorkshire, and French Acadians, who gorge into the bay. Gradually the flow slows down as the tide begins to rise again. At the tide's turn, the slack enables ships to pass the rapids before the flow builds up in the opposite direction. The bay's high tide of more than 14 ft above the river thrusts all the way inland to Fredericton, 135 km away. On your riverside walk in **Falls View Park,** try to ignore the pulp mill.

The bright new downtown area lovingly blends a modern and 19th-century atmosphere, especially along red-brick **King Street**. For all kinds of weather, skywalks and underground galleries link shopping and entertainment centres. **Market Square** is the attractive hub of the harbourfront renovation, a multilevel complex of shops, apartments, hotel and cafés, surrounding an atrium in what were once just ugly warehouses. At nearby **Barbour's General Store,** an authentic 19th-century grocery, try the local speciality of dulse, an edible seaweed that is New Brunswick's answer to chewing gum. It was at Market Slip that a contingent of 3,000 Loyalists landed in 1783 to found the city of Saint John. The event is commemorated in July by the Loyalists Days festival, with processions along the harbour and dancing in the streets, all performed in the costume of the 18th century.

New Brunswick Museum, 277 Douglas Avenue, is devoted principally to the province's grand old shipbuilding industry, source of considerable prosperity before timber had to bow to the new age of steam and steel. There are also interesting exhibits on the life of Micmac Indians and New Brunswick's animals and plants. The museum is currently being expanded and relocated to 1 Market Square. Work is expected to be completed in April 1996.

Bay of Fundy

Take Highway 1 north-east from Saint John and turn off at Penobsquis to head for **Fundy National Park,** a wonderful nature reserve with an emphasis on the seashore and its spectacular high tides. At the park entrance, you can get detailed maps of the 100 km of hiking trails linking campgrounds and chalets inside the park. If you are keen on golf, there is a 9-hole course with pathways for power carts. On Bennett Lake, you can rent a canoe or fish from a rowboat. On the shore, walk along the flats at low tide to seek out periwinkles, barnacles and sea anemones underneath the rocks. Herring

After hiking and biking along the cliffs of New Brunswick, the next challenge is the Atlantic itself.

Cove gives you a good view and detailed explanations of the tides.

Take a side-trip to **Hopewell Cape** at the mouth of the Petitcodiac River. If you can, camp overnight, as dawn is the perfect time to enjoy the view of its red cliffs and bizarre pillars of granite topped with tufts of balsam fir and black spruce, revealed at low tide. The rocks have been buffeted into what the tourist office calls flowerpots, but to children they look more like half-licked ice-cream cones.

Fredericton

New Brunswick's capital is a pleasant, sleepy little town most notable for the splendid **Beaverbrook Art Gallery**. It was built by William Maxwell Aitken (1879–1964), who as Lord Beaverbrook became a great British press baron and a member of Winston Churchill's war cabinet. (Although born in Ontario, he took his title from his home in Beaverbrook, New Brunswick.) Look out for Graham Sutherland's imposing portrait of the publisher of London's *Daily Express* and other fiercely patriotic newspapers. But the gallery's masterpiece is Salvador Dali's *Santiago el Grande*. Other important works include the English school of Reynolds, Gainsborough and Romney, and Canadian paintings by Tom Thomson,

Emily Carr and Cornelius Krieghoff.

The mid-19th-century neo-Gothic **Christ Church Cathedral**, with fine stained-glass windows and wooden beams, seems transplanted straight from the English countryside. In keeping with this spirit is the **changing of the guard** that you can watch on summer mornings on Officers' Square.

Explore the Saint John River west of Fredericton on a pretty 37-km excursion out to **King's Landing**, a reconstitution of a characteristic Loyalist village at the end of the 18th century. Veterans of the King's American Dragoons established a logging and shipbuilding community here, and their tasks are re-enacted today with remarkable authenticity. The waterwheel-driven sawmill still operates, as do a theatre and an inn, the King's Head, serving old-fashioned meals.

NEWFOUNDLAND

Without detracting from the significance of Columbus's landing on the Bahamas, Newfoundland can lay a just claim to being the true beginning of Europe's adventure in North America. Anyone seeking to understand Canada's role in shaping North America should spare a few days for this bracing province of hardy fisherfolk—first Canadian land to be "found" and last to join the Confederation (incorporating Labrador in 1949). The land- and seascapes are impressively rugged and the spirited people a sheer delight. Life in isolated fishing communities has given the Newfies a keen sense of local identity. Citizens of the capital of St. John's are "townees", those on the outskirts "bay-

men"; and the towns beyond are "outports". "Canadian" is still reserved for a mainlander.

"Seek ye first the Kingdom of God," says the provincial motto. "But on your way, look out for Newfoundland," seems to have been the slogan of the old North Atlantic navigators, from the good Irish Abbot Brendan in the 6th century and the wild Norsemen in the 11th, to all the Basque, French, Spanish and Portuguese fishermen who preceded explorer John Cabot. Cabot was paid £10 by Henry VII for finding "the new isle" in 1497.

It was the fishermen who really knew what the island was worth—the Grand Banks to the east of Newfoundland are the richest breeding ground of cod in the world, although they have become sadly denuded in recent years. For centuries, the island existed only for its offshore fish. Any permanent settlement was actively discouraged, so as not to compete with Britain's West Country merchants. Even after the first serious colonization of the 18th century, the interior was merely a source of wood for fisherman's cottages and ships.

Courage in a Curragh

You don't believe a 6th-century abbot and company of monks could cross the Atlantic from Ireland to Newfoundland in a 36-foot ox-hide curragh? Well, consider this: researchers of the medieval text of the Voyage of St. Brendan, taking into account the prevailing winds and currents, conclude that Abbot Brendan first sailed north from Ireland to the Hebrides, then took a stepping-stone course to the Faeroe Islands and across to Iceland then Greenland. Another stage from west Greenland to Baffin Island and it would be a cinch for the monks to sail with the current down the Labrador coast to Newfoundland. The conclusion is that Brendan, even on the longest haul between the Faeroes and Iceland, could have made the voyage without ever being more than 200 miles from land. Assuming of course that the abbot added to his saintly fortitude the navigational abilities of an admiral.

St. John's

Local folklore insists that the name (not to be confused with Saint John, New Brunswick) comes from the saint's day of

John the Baptist, June 24, when John Cabot arrived there in 1497.

Newfoundland's capital and largest city retains the simple allure of the fishing port it has always been, and the picturesque **harbour** is the obvious place to begin your sightseeing tour. In the 19th century, the town burned down five times, but it still stubbornly builds wooden houses overlooking the waterfront. Their brightly painted walls add a welcome touch of colour to the gaunt grey trawlers in the docks: from Britain, of course, but also from the former Soviet Union and even Japan. Parallel to the harbour, you should look for **Gower Street** where you'll find the prettiest Victorian houses, painted burgundy, lemon, burnt sienna, dove grey and white.

Newfoundland Museum, on Duckworth Street, recounts the human history of the island, displaying the dwellings and artefacts of the Inuit and Indians, including the now extinct Beothuk. Natural history and military exhibitions are now permanent features as well, while another part of the museum is devoted to the province's colourful seafaring history.

Safely up on a hill on Military Road, the Catholic **Basilica of St. John the Baptist** (1850) escaped the numerous fires to dominate the town's skyline with its granite and limestone towers. Down on Gower Street, the **Anglican cathedral**, also named after John the Baptist, burned down twice, and its simple neo-

Houses in St. John's, Newfoundland, all seem to look out to sea, waiting for the fishermen to come home.

Gothic 20th-century version is still without a steeple.

For the best view of the harbour go up to **Signal Hill**, looking over the narrows and out to the Atlantic Ocean. The hill was fortified to guard the harbour entrance during the Napoleonic Wars, and you can still see cannon of the Queen's Battery, installed in 1796. The **Cabot Tower** was built in 1897, fourth cen-

tenary of Cabot's landing and diamond jubilee of Queen Victoria. Four years later, at 12.30 p.m., December 12, 1901, in a receiving station improvised near the tower in a hospital (burned down in 1920), Guglielmo Marconi suddenly yelled: "Do you hear that? Do your hear that?" What the Italian inventor was so excited about were three faint dots of the letter S in Morse,

141

from his transmitter in Poldhu, Cornwall. The group of dour Newfie fishermen listening in were more impressed by this fellow jumping up and down than by history's first transatlantic radio message. The event is commemorated by a modest exhibit in the Cabot Tower.

On the north side of the hill, **Quidi Vidi** (pronounced Kiddy Viddy) is a charming little fishing port with excellent seafood restaurants. On the first Wednesday in August, St. John's Regatta, a race for six-oar rowing boats, is held on Quidi Vidi Lake. Begun in the 1820s, this oldest continuing sporting event in North America is also the occasion of a boisterous carnival.

Avalon Peninsula

The drive south down the peninsula from St. John's takes you first out to **Cape Spear**, a windswept rocky promontory jutting out into the crashing waves of the Atlantic—easternmost point of North America (longitude 52° 37′ 24″). More than an idle statistic, this strategic position prompted the Americans to install two anti-submarine gun emplacements on the tip of the cape in World War II. The 1835 white clapboard **lighthouse** there has been restored with a jolly red and white striped dome, while a less attractive modern concrete tower does all the work.

Down at the bird sanctuary on **Witless Bay**, you can spot pen-

---

Talking Newfie

Remote from the rest of Canada, the good people of Newfoundland have an accent that makes some think of the rustic folk in a school production of Shakespeare. There's a southern Irish brogue to the speech you'll hear around St. John's, while elsewhere the English has something of a Dorset or Devon twang.

As for the vocabulary, when you hear of a binicky angishore *bostooning about his* crubeens *and* screech, *you should know, of course, that an ill-tempered wretch has been complaining about his pickled pigs' feet and rum. If he's*

glutching *(swallowing with difficulty), don't* crossackle *(vex) him with too much* plaumaush *(soft talk), just give him a* bannikin *of* switchel *(tin cup of cold tea) to settle his* puddock *(stomach).*

And keep away from any drung *(narrow, rocky lane) when it's* mauzy *(misty), you may find yourself* clumming *with a* scut *(grappling with a dirty trouble-maker). It's sometimes safer to be a* shooneen *(coward).*

As the Newfie proverb has it, "You can't tell the mind of a squid"—beware of unreliable people—and "Long may your big jib draw"—good luck!

guins, puffins, guillemots and little auks. Best sightings are from mid-June to mid-July, when you can hire a boat from Bay Bulls out to **Gull Island**.

Nowadays, it's rare to see Newfies use the old Norse method for drying the cod.

Marine Drive north of St. John's takes you up a characteristically craggy coast through the fishing villages of Outer Cove, Middle Cove and Torbay up to pretty Pouch Cove. Look out for the whales that pass down this coast in summer. On the shore, you might see the wooden trestled racks on which a few fishermen still dry the cod in the traditional manner. For a view of Newfoundland at its wildest and most magnificently desolate, drive beyond Marine Drive on the gravel road leading to Cape St. Francis.

BRITISH COLUMBIA

"Such a land," said Rudyard Kipling in 1908, "is good for an energetic man. It is also not bad for a loafer." That's still true today.

British Columbia is supremely the land of the wild outdoors, with the constant challenge of rugged mountains, seemingly impenetrable forests, a jagged coastline and dizzily fast-moving rivers. But its capital is the smiling, sleepy town of Victoria, evoking a genteel British past that the British themselves may well have forgotten. And the province's principal city, with a population of over 1,700,000, is the beautifully situated Vancouver, home of easy living, elegant architecture and all the colour and movement of an international port. Loafers love it.

Long after Northwest Coast Indians had found the region to be a hospitable land of plenty, it was explored and "worked" by Scottish fur traders who called it New Caledonia. When the discovery of gold on the Fraser River in 1857 brought in a flood of American adventurers, Britain decided it was time to take the land over from the Hudson's Bay Company and create the colony of British Columbia. It joined the Dominion of Canada in 1871 on the understanding that the Canadian Pacific Railway would reach B.C. in the next decade (delay nearly caused secession). The C.P.R. choice of Vancouver as its terminus gave B.C. its major Pacific port.

The great boon of British Columbia, at least in the south-west corner where three-quarters of the population is clustered, is its gentle, relatively mild (but rainy) winters. B.C.'s kind weather has been a major factor in attracting new blood in the westward expansion from Ontario, Quebec and the Maritimes.

Trees are the main source of B.C.'s prosperity. The spruce, fir and cedar provide 58% of Canada's softwood lumber and 86% of its softwood plywood. By volume, B.C. is the world's largest exporter of softwood lumber.

Much to the joy of sports fishermen, the salmon of the Pacific coast and the great rivers of the interior remains another vital natural resource. The threat of overfishing has been cut back and, in a province where revenues from hydroelectric power are second only to those of Quebec, the energy industry has been prevented from damming the Fraser so as not to damage the salmon's spawning grounds.

B.C.'s population (3,668,400) is concentrated around the Strait of Georgia and along the American border, with scarcely any inhabitants at all north of Prince George. The people are still mainly British in origin, most of them Scottish. Other European immigrants are German, Dutch, Ukrainian, Italian, Scandinavian and a few French. Native Indians number about 170,000. From across the Pacific, the province has attracted a large Asian community—Chinese, Japanese and, of more recent arrival, Vietnamese, Pakistanis and Indians.

VANCOUVER

The city's setting in a magnificent bay embraced by soaring green mountains is one of those blessings that can turn any hard-boiled atheist into a believer. Cynicism dissolves with your first taste of the town's gentle ambience, created by a clever combination of the comforts of sophisticated modernity with the simpler joys of the wilderness at its back door.

Expanding at a purposeful but more leisurely pace than other leading Canadian cities, Vancouver has never lost sight of the importance of enjoying life at the same time. Many a bustling businessman from Toronto has been driven close to apoplexy by the relaxed style of his Vancouver colleagues. "With the difference in time zones," as one hard-working Vancouver banker has observed, "these Toronto guys are convinced we close down the same time as they do and work three hours a day less. It's not true, but it's not a bad idea."

In keeping with this easy-going attitude, the city was originally known as Gastown, after saloon-keeper "Gassy Jack" Deighton, who looked after the needs of pioneer lumbermen and sailors in the 1860s. It was only when it became C.P.R.'s west coast railway terminus in 1886 that it took on the more dignified name of one of the region's first European visitors, navigator George Vancouver. A fire in 1886 and modern property-developers left few traces of the 19th-century town, but bold contemporary architecture downtown and out at the Simon Fraser and University of British Columbia campuses blends beautifully with the mountain and ocean backdrop. Preparations for the world's fair of Expo '86 provided the impetus to clean up unsightly docklands, build handsome new housing on the waterfront and retain Canada Place as a proud new city symbol.

First View

More than in most towns, Vancouver's unique setting demands a carefully planned first view. The city is built around the broad English Bay which funnels through First and Second Narrows into the Burrard Inlet, which George Vancouver explored in a scouting boat in 1791. The harbour separates the city proper, with the Stanley Park promontory, from its elegant north shore mountainside suburbs of West and North Vancouver. To take in all this, you need to begin from not one, but two observation points.

Cross the First Narrows on Lions Gate Bridge and take the Capilano Road for a cable-car ride up to **Grouse Mountain** and its grand view south over the city and harbour. Try to be there at sunset, too, to see the city light up. A favourite with skiers, the mountain also offers a fine view north-west over Capilano Lake and across to Vancouver Island. If you feel like a quick whiff of the wilderness on your way back, turn off to walk the swaying suspension bridge 230 ft above the fast-flowing waters of **Capilano Canyon**.

To get an equally impressive view of the city set against its mountains, go downtown to the observation deck (and its restaurant, if you like) on top of the 40-storey **Harbour Centre** (555 West Hastings Street). A bonus on clear days is a view south, with the long-range telescope, of Mount Baker across the American border in the state of Washington.

Downtown

The main streets through the West End peninsula to Stanley Park are Georgia and Robson. Georgia Street continues through the park to Lion's Gate Bridge. Though you will need a car in this sprawling city, park it for your downtown tour and walk—traffic jams can be horrendous.

Start your tour of the city centre at Robson Square, site of one of the true masterpieces of modern North American architecture, Arthur Erickson's **Courthouse**. Characteristic of the Vancouver architect's finest works, the building is conceived horizontally, only seven storeys high but still the dominant focus among the skyscrapers towering above it. Revolutionizing the whole stuffy concept of law courts, with not a marble column or portico in sight, this sparkling structure spreads out in tiers of glassed-in walkways, offices and courtrooms, and also shops, restaurants, a small cinema and skating-rink. Pools cascade from one level to another among indoor and outdoor gardens of flowering shrubs and rose bushes, Japanese maples, orange trees and a miniature pine forest. An intriguing pattern of stairways and ramps collectively dubbed "stramps"—very popular with rollerskaters—runs across the plazas from corner to corner, attracting large crowds during city celebrations.

Robson Square also provides a home for **Vancouver Art Gallery** in the old courthouse (a proper neoclassical temple renovated by Erickson). The temporary exhibitions here sometimes feature the work of Canadian artist Emily Carr (1871–1945).

"Crazy Old Millie" as she was known locally—"Klee Wyck" or the "Laughing One" to her Kwakiutl Indian friends—was a popular eccentric in Victoria, where she kept a boarding house and wheeled a pet monkey around in a pram. Years of painting among the Indians and studying with French Post-Impressionists produced a unique style of vigorous, expressive landscapes and totemic themes achieved with great sweeps and swirls of bold colour. You may see the lush, dramatic *Big Raven* (1928) and *Forest, British Columbia* (1932) in which the trees have the sculptural quality of totem poles.

The section of Robson Street between Burrard and Bute streets is known as **Robsonstrasse**. Now it has lost its distinctively German character to become a cosmopolitan restaurant row offering Vietnamese, Japanese, Scandinavian, Italian and French cuisine.

East of Robson Square, the **Granville Mall** pedestrian shopping zone takes you down to the Harbour Centre and the waterfront. From the foot of Granville Street, take a bargain cruise on the commuter **Seabus** which crosses Burrard Inlet to North Vancouver, 12 minutes each way. Besides the "fish-eye view" of the city and harbour, you get a close-up of the grand **Canada Place**, jutting out into the harbour like an ocean liner, with a hint of the port's 19th-century beginnings in its white simulated sails. Originally the national pavilion at Expo '86, it is now the Vancouver Trade & Convention Centre.

If you don't have a taste for the down-and-out life of Skid Row on Hastings Street, make your way east to the brighter colours of **Chinatown** along Pender Street. Descendants of those that settled here after working on the Canadian Pacific Railway, Canada's largest Chinese community is cheerful at play in the *mahjong* parlours and earnest at work in the fruit and vegetable markets, fish-stalls, boutiques of silks and satins, bamboo and lacquer wares from Hong Kong, Taiwan and mainland China. Look out for the shops of traditional spices and medicines, where reindeer horn and deer's tail-tips are said to perk up even the weariest husband. Barbecued pork and poultry glisten in the windows of the dozens of restaurants, and tourists are drawn in by the garish street décor—even the telephone booths have pagoda-style roofs.

Away from the throngs, the **Dr. Sun Yat-Sen Garden**, at the corner of Carrall and Pender Streets, offers a rare moment of peace. This microcosm of nature reflecting the Taoist philosophy of yin and yang was landscaped by artists brought in from Suzhou, the great centre of classical Chinese gardens. A pavilion with a diversity of glazed roof tiles, carved woodwork and lattice windows overlooks a subtly patterned pebblestone courtyard and the miniature landscape. Light is balanced by shadow, rugged limestone rocks (yang) are chosen for their pitted and convoluted surface, balancing the smooth surface of calm pools and quiet streams (yin). Shrubs symbolize human virtues: pine, bamboo and winter-blooming plum represent strength, grace and the renewal of life.

Duly renewed, then, make your way towards the harbour and railyards, to **Gastown** (between Water and Hastings), the resuscitated red-brick, cobbled-street district of Vancouver's beginnings. This huckster's paradise of boutiques, souvenir shops, bars and restaurants is frankly commercial in its polished quaintness, but with a certain corny charm. At the west end of Water Street is the world's first (and probably only) monumental **steam-powered clock**, signalling the hours with a resounding whistle. On Maple Street, a no less handsome **statue** of Gassy Jack, a distinctly derelict-looking riverboat captain known to his mother as John Deighton, stands on a whisky barrel symbolizing the drinks he served to lumbermen, persuading them to build the town in 1867.

Escape the crowds by heading east along the waterfront to the docks where you used to be able to watch the ocean-going fishermen unloading their haul or join them for a hearty meal in the local canteen. And if the Robson Square Courthouse whetted your appetite for the architecture of Arthur Erickson, continue this side trip out along Hastings Street towards Burnaby Mountain (actually only 1,200 ft high) and the striking campus

An island of tranquillity at Chinatown's Sun Yat-Sen Garden.

of **Simon Fraser University**. The spectacular focus of student activity is the great mall of the Academic Quadrangle. Note the delicate play of light and shadow among stairways and terraces under the mall's truss-supported glass roof. On the way back downtown, swing over to the **B.C. Place**, a vast concrete oval-domed sports stadium where the B.C. Lions play their football indoors.

If you need any more information about Greater Vancouver, Vancouver Tourism can offer plenty of help and advice. Their office is at 200 Burrard Street.

Stanley Park

On its magnificent peninsula proudly dominating English Bay, this is undoubtedly one of North America's finest city parks. Its forest of majestic Douglas firs, cedars and Sitka spruce remind us it was once a government reserve providing mast and spar timbers for the Royal Navy. At the turn of the century, the town leased it as a park, named after Lord Stanley, Canada's governor general. His bronze statue is close to the southern entrance.

Turn east off Georgia Street to take the 9-km drive looping the park. More bracing is the **Sea Wall Promenade**, where you can walk, jog or ride a bicycle (available for rent on Denman Street).

Passing the immaculate green playing field of Brockton Oval, you may spot a cricket game, reminding you this is *British* Columbia. A splendid group of Haida and Kwakiutl totem poles nearby illustrate the province's other important cultural influence. On your way to Brockton Point, look out for the 9 o'clock gun, a cannon that fires at 9 p.m., originally in order to warn fishermen of the fishing curfew.

Turning west, you'll pass on the seaward side a bronze statue oddly named Girl in a Wet Suit, a version of Copenhagen's mermaid designed not to shock. Stop off at **Prospect Point** for a good view of oil tankers and grain cargo ships bound for Japan, China or the former Soviet Union. A totem pole marks the site where Captain Vancouver met with members of the Squamish tribe.

At the **Aquarium**, besides the dolphin show, star attractions are killer and beluga whales, closely followed by sharks. But equally scary are wolf-eels with crab-cracking jaws.

You can walk marked trails to picnic at the pretty freshwater **Beaver Lake**, from which the beavers were "deported" after creating havoc with the water system. The park's popular sandy **beaches** run along the west shore of the peninsula.

English Bay

Get away from the city centre with an excursion out to **Point Grey**. You can relax on the pleasant beaches; Wreck Beach is reserved for nudists. But more seriously, explore the grounds of the **University of British Columbia**, one of the most beautiful college campuses in North America. The terraced Sedgwick Library and the Faculty Club rose garden are two notable gems set against a superb sea and mountain backdrop.

The university's pride and joy is the great **Museum of Anthropology** out on Marine Drive at Point Grey. Arthur Erickson designed this noble glass and concrete-beam structure in 1972 as an explicit homage to the post-and-beam longhouses of the Northwest Coast Indians. Gracing the lawns are a magnificent group of **totem poles** and two **cedarwood houses** of the Haida Indians, built in the 1930s faithful to a centuries-old technique and form.

Inside the museum, alongside the artefacts of other Pacific civilizations, the rich culture of the coastal tribes—Haida, Kwakiutl, Salish, Tlingit and Tsimshian—is beautifully displayed and illuminated in a space where the roof-glass seems to open the halls to the heavens. Compare the sturdy **cedarwood canoes**, built to negotiate the Pacific's coastal waters, with the lighter birchbark craft used by Eastern Woodlands Indians for the rivers of Ontario and Quebec.

Many of the **sculptures** you see were incorporated into the structure of a house as posts and cross-beams. One Kwakiutl giant accompanied by two slaves, emphasizing the house-owner's power and prestige, originally supported a massive central roof beam. Others represent the tribes' totemic animals, such as the bear, protecting a human being in his bosom. Prehistoric stone carvings show the continuity of totemic styles. Some smaller figures, in soft black argillite stone, were turned out by Haida craftsmen specifically for 19th-century European tourists who found themselves "caricatured" in the carvings.

Look out for the huge wooden feast dishes, big as bathtubs, for dispensing food at the great "potlatch" ceremonies at which the tribes proclaimed their greatness by the munificence of their hospitality (see p. 39). An important part of the collection is devoted to gold, silver and copper **jewellery** and wooden **masks** and **ceremonial rattles**. Many of these are kept in Galleries 6 and 7, but don't hurry past just because they look like the museum's store rooms. That's what they are, but this so-called **visible storage system** is a major innova-

tion to make permanently available the museum's thousands of art objects. Here you're encouraged to make your own discoveries, compare the work of different cultures around the world, but also just admire the sheer wealth of allegedly "primitive" creativity.

Just to the south of the museum, the **Nitobe Memorial Gardens** are a fine example of classical Japanese landscaping.

Stone-lanterned paths lead you across hump-bridged ponds to a traditional teahouse set among Japanese maples and azaleas. B.C.'s Pacific-oriented involvement is further emphasized at the nearby **Asian Centre**, which holds interesting exhibitions of the art, costumes and photographs of China, Japan, India, Korea and Indonesia.

Return to the city centre on Point Grey Road and stop off

near Jericho Beach to visit the **Old Hastings Mill Store**, 1575 Alma Road. Carried here lock, stock and barrel from downtown in the 1930s, this is the town's oldest surviving building, post office, general store and only remnant from the original Gastown to have escaped the 1886 fire. It has been restored as a museum for turn-of-the-century paraphernalia. Closest that wholesome Vancouverites get to

In Vancouver, work and pleasure mix easily—boats moored near the business district for a quick getaway.

being Bohemian, the **Kitsilano** neighbourhood here is popular with students, young and old. The artists tend to gather around Commercial Drive.

In the little Vanier Park by the Burrard Bridge, you'll find two interesting little museums and the Pacific Space Centre. The

Centennial Museum is devoted to local history and anthropology. The **Maritime Museum** traces the history of the Pacific port, with its showpiece the *Saint-Roch*, proud ship of the Royal Canadian Mounted Police which sailed clear around the North American continent via the Panama Canal and the Arctic Ocean, to plot a definitive Northwest Passage and hunt German U-boats on the way.

The area where English Bay narrows into False Creek epitomizes Vancouver's taste for the good life. The once miserable wasteland of run-down warehouses, lumber-mills, factories and railyards has been reclaimed

Lumberjacks bet their bottom dollar at annual Squamish logging contest.

not only for the upbeat commercial enterprises that are now a familiar feature of any Canadian city with a waterfront, but also as a handsome residential neighbourhood. Under the Granville Bridge, **Granville Island** (really a triangular peninsula of landfill) is a cheerful collection of markets, cafés, galleries, boutiques and theatres. Children love it not just for the toys in Kids Only Market but also for the water playground around the fire hydrants and tons of rubber tyres.

False Creek has given its name to a charming neighbourhood of architecturally inventive houses set around garden-courtyards and terraces. The east end of the "creek" was the site of Expo '86, perpetuated by the giant geodesic dome of **Expo Centre**, now home to **Science World** and The **Omnimax Theatre**.

"Timber-r-r-r!"

Today's lumberjack ain't what he used to be. In the good old days, he hiked his way out to British Columbia's endless wilderness to hole up for six months at a time in isolated lumber camps in a gloomy windowless log cabin, emerging only to chop down everything in sight, stripping whole forests bare. "Cut and run", it was called. He shaved with his axe as a razor, ate salt pork and beans for lunch and beans and salt pork for dinner. Women were barred from camp because, it was said, he might get distracted and chop off a finger.

Now he commutes to the forest in a station wagon, fells his quota of trees with a power saw, as carefully directed by forestry scientists who have selected the trees by computer-programmed surveys, and then drives home each night to his house in the suburbs. You can't shave with a power saw.

155

SQUAMISH HIGHWAY

The drive over Lions Gate Bridge to Vancouver's **North Shore** suburbs along Marine Drive and the Upper Levels Highway (Route 99) makes a gentle introduction to your exploration of the Pacific coast and interior. With a view of the ocean from a setting of tall Douglas firs and red cedars among boulders, and the occasional swift mountain stream, the elegant or rustic houses enjoy a civilized microcosm of the classical B.C. landscape.

Route 99 turns north at Horseshoe Bay (landing-stage for the Vancouver Island ferry) to become the Squamish Highway for a spectacular 100-km drive up to Whistler Mountain. The Coastal Mountains come right down to the water's edge of the narrow **Howe Sound**, some forming a little archipelago in the sea.

Stop off at **Shannon Falls**, a short walk away from the road on an easy gravel path over footbridges into the forest. You can picnic at the bottom of the cliff over which the water cascades. Famous for its August log-rolling contests, the town of **Squamish** makes a useful base for hiking tours into Garibaldi Provincial Park. The new winter sports resort of **Whistler** offers excellent summer facilities, too: bicycles, kayak and river-rafting or more sedate swimming, golf and tennis. Take the ski-lift for

views across the Coastal Mountains or stroll around **Lost Lake** —good trout-fishing—but beware of a pretty yellow flower known as skunk cabbage that smells like its name when you pick it.

As a delightful alternative to driving, you can travel from Vancouver to Squamish aboard the **Royal Hudson 2860** steam train, a regular old puffer giving you a close-up view of mountain and forest. The round trip takes 6 hours, including a 2-hour stopover in Squamish allowing for a walk over to Shannon Falls. You also have the option of making one leg of the trip by sea, 30 minutes longer. Board the morning train in North Vancouver at the bottom of Pemberton Avenue and return from Squamish on the *MV Britannia* ferry—or vice versa, starting from Vancouver's Harbour Ferry dock at the bottom of Denman Street.

VICTORIA

Probably the most genteel city in all of North America, this town is of another age, another world. In its sheltered spot on the southeast tip of Vancouver Island, flowers seem to be growing everywhere. Geraniums in baskets hanging from five-bulb lamp-posts in the city's shopping streets; hydrangeas and roses in the lovingly tended gardens of the residential neighbourhoods;

shrubs and more exotic blooms in the city's parks and conservatories.

In the month of February, while the rest of Canada is still huddled around log fires and radiators, even just across the Strait of Georgia in Vancouver, the people of Victoria are out in their parks and gardens for the annual flower-count. Yes, they count every blossom in town, and the figure for 1995 was nearly 4 billion. For Victoria is blessed with an exceptionally mild climate, with enough rain to water the flowers, but an annual average (they count everything in this town) of 2,183 hours of sun to give them their brilliant colours. Even the air in Victoria is sweet and gentle.

Not surprisingly in a town attracting an affluent retirement community, the port is more pleasure- than work-oriented, filling its harbours with cruise liners and yachts, ferries and seaplanes. Parliament reminds the citizenry of the town's venerable past and more serious role as B.C.'s legislative capital. Not that it detracts from the hallowed ritual of tea-time, act of obeisance to a more legendary than real Britain. Good for a chuckle, but if it highlights Victoria's resistance to the rest of the planet's hustle and bustle, so much the better.

The town is small enough to get around most of it on foot, but there are also horse-drawn carriages and red double-decker buses from London. The toy-like quality of Victoria is emphasized in its most imposing building, the **Parliament**. Built in 1897, it was certainly erected by someone with a playful sense of what might best evoke merrie olde England. There's a little bit of London's St. Paul's Cathedral in the massive central dome topped, for want of a saint, by a gilded statue of Captain George Vancouver. The neo-Romanesque arched entrance recalls the British capital's Natural Science Museum, and the smaller-domed turrets suggest something between an Englishman's castle and his county council. The whole fairytale effect is enhanced at night when every contour of the Parliament is outlined by thousands of light bulbs.

Inside, you can visit the debating chamber, unmistakably modelled on the House of Commons. In the great dome's interior **rotunda**, painter George Southwell's murals illustrate the four virtues that "made" British Columbia: Courage, as shown by George Vancouver confronting the Spanish at Nootka Sound in 1792; Spirit of Enterprise, with James Douglas establishing Fort Victoria for the Hudson's Bay Company in 1842; Work, by those who had to build the Fort; and Justice, meted out to the unruly mob engaged in the 1858 gold rush.

Reasonably enough, the Parliament grounds include a bronze statue of Queen Victoria. It was she who chose the name of British Columbia—over New Caledonia, New Hanover, New Cornwall or New Georgia. There is also a **cenotaph** which commemorates soldiers who were killed in the Battle of Britain. You can easily get the impression that this town is only nominally in Canada.

Immediately east of the Parliament is the newly housed **Provincial Museum**, devoted to B.C.'s fauna, flora and a first-rate collection of Indian art. In front of the museum stands the 62-bell **Netherlands Carillon Tower**, a gift of Dutch-Canadians and tallest bell-tower in the country.

Further east is **Thunderbird Park**, home of the city's most important collection of Indian carvings—Tsimshian and Haida totem poles, Salish sculpture of their chieftains and a reconstructed Kwakiutl longhouse. The thunderbird, a mythical creature whose eyes flashed the lightning and whose beating wings rumbled the thunder, figures in many of the carvings in the park. At the sculpture workshop, you can see Indians still practising the ancient skills but with modern tools. Most of the park's wood carvings date from the last half of the 19th century, but are restored and replaced when weather or worms get the better of them.

At the corner of Dallas Road and Douglas Street is Kilometre 0 of the 7,800-km Trans-Canada Highway (ending up, with the aid of a ferry or two, in St. John's, Newfoundland).

It is here that the flowers and greenery of Victoria begin their most delightful assault, in **Beacon Hill Park**, an expanse of gently rolling flower-bordered lawns and groves of cedar and oak sloping down to the Pacific Ocean. Look out for the 114-ft totem pole carved by Chief Mungo Martin and believed to be the tallest in existence.

At the northern end of Beacon Hill is the **Crystal Gardens** conservatory. You can have tea on the Upper Terrace overlooking tropical plants, exotic birds and repulsive reptiles. They are kept well away for the monthly ballroom dancing sessions.

The **Empress Hotel**, further north, is so prestigious and renowned for its elegant servings of tea that it schedules three separate afternoon sittings every day, and you're advised to make

The double-decker buses come from Piccadilly Circus, but the ivy on the Empress Hotel is home-grown.

a reservation if you want to participate in the ritual. The Empress was built in 1908 to serve passengers ferried across from the western terminus of the Canadian Pacific and is the archetypal grand old railway hotel.

There's a good replica of Victoria looking decidedly unamused in the **Royal London Wax Museum** (Belleville Street, near the Inner Harbour). Charles and Di are a little more cheerful.

The **Inner Harbour** is a pleasant place for loitering among the yachts and seaplanes. The harbour's **Pacific Undersea Gardens** is an unusually well-presented natural aquarium that you view from beneath the sea. Besides the exquisite tropical specimens, there's a perfectly horrid giant octopus.

The **Maritime Museum** in the old courthouse on Bastion Square contains some fine models and navigational paraphernalia of the merchant ships of yore—whalers, steamers and old Hudson's Bay paddle-wheelers. The star attraction is the original *Tilikum*, a 40-ft dugout canoe that was equipped with three sails to take Captain J.C. Voss in 1901 on a crazy three-year voyage round the world. He sailed from Victoria via Australia, New Zealand, Brazil, the

Another hectic day for the locals down at the Victoria bowling-green.

Cape of Good Hope and the Azores to land up in the English seaside town of Margate.

The **Emily Carr Gallery** (1107 Wharf Street) presents changing exhibitions of Victoria's best-known painter (see p. 147), along with memorabilia and a short

---

From Here to Eternity

Victoria provokes some strange reactions in its visitors. Rudyard Kipling came here in 1907 and, with the insouciant snobbery of the incorrigible place-dropper, he wrote home: "To realise Victoria you must take all that the eye admires most in Bournemouth, Torquay, the Isle of Wight, the Happy Valley at Hong Kong, the Doon, Sorrento and Camps Bay; add reminiscences of the Thousand Islands, and arrange the whole around the Bay of Naples, with some Himalayas for the background."

Bemused by the town's appeal to senior citizens, B.C. bar-room wags insist: "Victoria is God's waiting room. It is the only cemetery in the world with street lighting." This view was shared by Stephen Leacock, Canadian economist and humorist, who said in a 1936 speech, from the safety of Vancouver: "In Victoria the people turn over in the morning to read the daily obituary column. Those who do not find their names there fall back and go to sleep again."

film about her life and work. The town's **Art Gallery** (Wilspencer Place, south of Fort Street) has works of the English Impressionist Walter Sickert, French water-colourist Eugène Boudin and Dutch landscape-painter of the 17th century, Adriaen van de Velde.

Drive 22 km north of town to a veritable floral fairyland, **Butchart Gardens.** Robert Pim Butchart made a fortune out of Portland cement at the turn of the century and found himself stuck with an exhausted limestone quarry. His wife suggested turning the whole thing into a garden. The result is an almost bewilderingly beautiful phantasmagoria of fountains, lakes, rockeries, trees and flowers: the **Sunken Garden**, with symmetrical Trees of Life and rockery of gentian, saxifrage and Lebanon candytuft; the **Rose Garden**, at its best in July, boasting 200 varieties of hybrid tea and floribunda roses; the **Japanese Gardens**, with scarlet azaleas, Himalayan blue poppies, weeping larch and pond with a couple of cranes to bring you good luck; and the dreamy **Italian Garden**, cypresses singing a song of Tuscany around a cruciform basin filled with water lilies where once was Mr. and Mrs. Butchart's tennis court. The gardens also put on firework displays and open-air theatre.

VANCOUVER ISLAND

Some 460 km long and averaging 80 km wide, the mountainous island is covered by the largest stand of lumber in the world, a boon to the province's most important industry, but also a magnet for nature-lovers. They hike or flyfish for trout in the interior and then make for the superb sandy beaches along the island's west coast, to picnic or troll for Pacific salmon. For several thousand years, it has been a favoured spot for Indian hunters and fishermen living around the sheltered coves and fjords that penetrate deep inland. Today, about 7,000 Salish and Wakash Indians still live on the island, well away from the towns and tourist resorts.

Coming from Vancouver, board the car ferry at Horseshoe Bay for Nanaimo and head north on Highway 19. Turn west at Parksville to cross the island on Highway 4. This takes you through some of the province's finest forestland: the red cedar of Indians' canoes, totem poles and longhouses; stately Douglas fir, mainstay of white man's bridges, boats, houses and flagstaffs; and the good old Sitka spruce Christmas tree.

About 20 km from Parksville,

Boardwalks make the going easy among the Douglas firs of Cathedral Grove.

look out for a signpost to **Little Qualicum Falls**. The exhilarating, well-marked walk loops around the upper falls tumbling into a ravine, then follows the river rapids along to the lower falls that crash into another rocky gorge. You can also drive a short distance for a picnic or bracing swim at **Cameron Lake**.

Highway 4 follows the lake shore to **Cathedral Grove**, a formidable stand of Douglas firs in MacMillan Provincial Park, donated to the public by a paper manufacturer as a gesture for government permission to exploit less accessible parts of the forest. Many of the firs, up to 230 ft high, are more than 300 years old, the most ancient dating back to the 12th century. Excellent explanatory panels trace the growth of these majestic trees. Off the beaten track, you'll steep yourself in the atmosphere of a truly primeval forest.

Stock up on picnic supplies in the town of Port Alberni before driving on past Kennedy Lake and down to **Pacific Rim National Park**. Its sandy beaches are a delight, the powerful ocean-breakers being particularly admired by champion surfers. At the coast, Highway 4 turns north along one of the best resort areas, the self-explanatory **Long Beach**, 12 km of fine sand and first-class fishing waters. Hotels here provide you with cooking facilities for whatever fish you—or a generous neighbour—might catch. Boardwalk rambles along **Wickaninnish Bay** will take you in and out of the coastal pine forest. **Florencia Bay** is a good bathing beach, while **South Beach** is the mecca for

Far from the madding crowds on Vancouver Island's Long Beach.

164

collectors of "worry stones". These exquisite green, aubergine or (most prized of all) jet black pebbles are gathered from hidden nooks and crannies, sorted for size, shape and smoothness of texture until the ideal stone is located, a highly subjective appraisal. All others are discarded and the collector can be seen caressing the pebble, rubbing all worries away. From **Comber's Beach**, you can spot sea lions basking out on the rocks, with not a worry in the world.

For a change of pace, the sleepy town of **Tofino** is a community of ecologists, painters and poets pursuing a style of life remote in every sense from the B.C. mainstream. Take a look at the Indian art gallery and performances at the experimental theatre.

On the north-east coast of the island, departing from Port Hardy, B.C. Ferries organizes a daytime (summer) or overnight (winter) cruise through the spectacular **Inside Passage,** between the forested island coast and the nordic fjords of the B.C. mainland. Docking up in Prince Rupert harbour, you're likely to see a very cosmopolitan mixture of sailors—Greeks, Italians, Russians, Chinese, Sikh Indians, even a few British.

FRASER AND THOMPSON CANYONS

This stark mountain landscape of pine forest progressively thinning out to more arid, craggy canyons above the fast-flowing river is the pioneer country that "made" British Columbia. Driving east from Vancouver on the Trans-Canada Highway and following the Fraser River north to its tributary, the Thompson, you are backtracking along the great exploration route traced by

---

A Salmon Primer

Of the five species of Canada's Pacific salmon—sockeye, pink, coho, chum and chinook—the sockeye *is the most appreciated for its food value. Caught before spawning, it's bright red, rich in oil and holds its colour and flavour in processing.*

It spawns in tributary streams above a lake, and the hatched young or small fry makes its way down to the lake to grow on a diet of water fleas to a length of 3 to 4 inches. After one or two years, it's ready for the ocean, making a journey of up to 1,000 miles. Three summers at sea, feeding off shrimp, and it returns in autumn weighing 5 to 7 pounds to spawn in its native river. Battering its way upstream and leaping obstacles like Hell's Gate, the salmon instinctively seeks out the original stream where it began as an egg four years

earlier. At the spawning ground, the female scours a nest or "redd" with her tail and deposits some 3,500 pink-red eggs. The male, which has grown a hump and fierce hooked snout to fight off rivals during the mating period, sprays the eggs with his sperm. Within ten days the adults die, a grey shadow of their crimson prime. But in the gravel bed of the stream, the new cycle begins the following spring, when the young hatch and make their way down to the lake.

Sportsmen favour high-jumping coho *and fighting* chinook *(King Salmon to Americans), both weighing up to 25 pounds, with the chinook reaching 40 pounds after a fifth year. In this league, the* pink *is a minnow. The* chum, *also known as* dog, *contains less oil than the other species; it was easy to dry and stocked the Indians' larder during the winter months.*

166

intrepid fur traders from the prairies to the Pacific. It's also the route unerringly followed by millions of Pacific salmon between the ocean and their spawning grounds far inland. And, against all the odds of the terrain, it's the route the railways chose to carry the riches of lumber, mining—and the first tourists—across the continent.

One of the most impressive sights on your trip will be the rivalry of the Canadian Pacific and Canadian National railways in action: endless trains of freight wagons, pulled and pushed often by two engines at either end for the tougher stretches, snake through the canyons on opposite banks of the river.

Turn north at Hope to **Yale,** an old fort of the Hudson's Bay Company, terminus of its sternwheelers unable to negotiate the rapids upriver—at low water you can still see their ring tie-ups on the river bank. A little **museum** documents how this sleepy village of a few hundred inhabitants was once a gold rush boom town and the major construction depot for the C.P.R.

The strands of B.C.'s destiny come together where the Fraser Canyon narrows at the torrential rapids of **Hell's Gate**. For thousands of years, this point in the river's descent to the ocean was the local Indians' favoured fishing spot for the salmon swimming to their spawning grounds. It was here in 1808 that they helped Nor'Wester fur trader Simon Fraser with his canoe past the rapids, over a swaying ropeway of vines strung along the canyon wall, enabling him to follow the ocean the river that bears his name. In 1914, the C.N.R. blocked the salmon's passage with rock-blasts through the canyon for the railway. The consequent 90 per cent reduction of the annual sockeye salmon catch was remedied only 30 years later when multimillion-dollar steel-and-concrete channels were built for the fish. The Indians are back again unofficially, leaning far out over precarious rocky ledges to pluck with dip nets just a tiny amount of salmon, compared with the millions caught by the commercial fisheries at the Fraser estuary. Take the **cable-car** across the gorge for a close-up view of the rapids. For a taste of what the fuss is all about, try a grilled salmon lunch at the restaurant by the cable-car terminal.

The Thompson River joins the Fraser at **Lytton.** Before turning east on the Trans-Canada Highway to follow the Thompson, take a look (just north of town on Highway 12) at the dramatic effect of the **confluence** mixing the lime of the tributary with the clearer mountain waters of the

167

Fraser. The drier Thompson valley soon takes on a more rugged aspect than the Fraser, with the sagebrush and lizards of a semi-desert, in places as beautifully desolate as a moonscape. The similarity with America's southwest is reinforced by the ranches around **Kamloops Lake**.

If you're here in October, you may see the spectacular **salmon run**, when the waters turn scarlet with thousands of sockeye. Take the turn-off on the Trans-Canada at Squilax Bridge to the junction of the Adams River and Shuswap Lake. On the Thompson River, summer visitors can try the bumpy thrills of the sockeye experience for themselves with some whitewater river rafting organized out of Vancouver—details from the city tourist information office.

OKANAGAN VALLEY

Before heading east to the Rocky Mountains, turn south on Highway 97 to the lovely Okanagan resort country for golf, tennis, swimming, hiking, camping and fishing amid vineyards, orchards and dozens of trout lakes. The Okanagan River itself widens into an elongated lake with excellent sandy beaches, sailing and other water sports facilities centred around **Kelowna**.

Across the lake at **Westbank**, among other orchard towns, you pay for what you pick: apricots,

peaches, cherries, plums, pears and apples. At the southern end of the lake, the resort town of **Penticton** stages a Peach Festival in August.

Sunny Okanagan Valley is one of only two wine-growing areas in Canada (the other being in Niagara Peninsula, Ontario). 21 **wineries** propose tastings and sales of their not undrinkable dry whites and dry reds along with

some more refined wines from the nobler European varieties: Pinot Noir, Cabernet Sauvignon, Chardonnay, Gewürztraminer and Riesling. Among the several wineries you can visit in the area are Mission Hill in Westbank and Gray Monk at **Okanagan Centre.**

Hottest spot in the region, down by the American border, is **Osoyoos,** nestling in the mountains around a good swimming lake and pocket-sized but honest-to-goodness desert complete with cactus, sagebrush, rattlesnakes, coyotes and horned toads.

More than anything else, the railway made Canada.

THE ROCKIES AND PRAIRIES

In this region, the great Canadian outdoors really comes into its own. The national parks of the Rocky Mountains provide unrivalled opportunities for exhilarating contacts with a wilderness where you can really escape from your fellow man: camping and hiking through the forests; fishing in the myriad lakes and rivers; canoeing and whitewater rafting in the mountain torrents. And skiing, downhill and cross-country, has been greatly enhanced by the ultra-modern facilities installed for Calgary's 1988 Winter Olympics.

Alberta, Saskatchewan and Manitoba form the Prairie Provinces, sharing the same rugged climate. The full meaning of Canada's "wide open spaces" becomes instantly apparent here, in the vast stretches of wheat field reaching to the horizon. The eye is attracted not by some craggy obstacle but by the play of a sudden wind sweeping across the plain. The sky is the spectacle, offering magnificent dawns and sunsets. Play the farmers' game of watching the weather come and go.

Stop in the provincial capitals of Edmonton, Regina and Winnipeg for a glimpse of the region's history and culture. Monuments and museums show how the buffalo-hunting Métis, the descendants of Indians and French fur traders, struggled in vain against Anglo farmers from Ontario, themselves subsequently relayed by waves of Eastern European immigrants brought in to exploit the grain wealth of the prairies. One side-trip in Manitoba touches on another Canadian adventure, up to Churchill on Hudson Bay, the centre of the great fur trading company's northern activities. A bonus in autumn is the rare "southern" appearance of polar bears.

ROCKY MOUNTAINS

If there's one region for which you should reserve most of your superlatives and stock up on rolls of film, this is it. For all visitors to western Canada, whether they be sturdy backwoodsmen, skiers and mountaineers or more easy-going loafers seeking to rest their tired bones in a hot springs spa or bask beside a sparkling lake, the national parks of the Rocky

Mountains are an undisputed imperative.

Straddling the border of British Columbia and Alberta, the North American continent's grandest range of mountains stretches from the Yukon Territory down to the Mexican frontier. For the tourist, the abundance of superbly administered national parks—Mount Revelstoke, Glacier, Kootenay, Yoho, Banff and Jasper—give the Canadian Rockies an edge over their American counterpart, to which thousands of American visitors will testify. (Most of the national parks charge a nominal entrance fee—check at the park entrance, as you may be stopped by park-rangers later on. You can buy a four-day permit or an annual permit which admits the vehicle and occupants to all national parks.)

The stark drama of the mountain landscapes derives from the fact that, in geological terms, the Rockies were born "yesterday" and have not had the time to settle into more stable forms. Waves of sedimentary rock lifted by vast thrust faults less than 60 million years ago have created a variety of striking silhouettes: the battlements of a medieval fortress, sawteeth or single pyramids like the Swiss Matterhorn. The highest peak in the Canadian Rockies is Mount Robson, 12,850 ft, just inside B.C.

Mount Revelstoke

The highway through the Monashee and Selkirk mountains to Mount Revelstoke National Park follows the Eagle River and the route of the C.P.R. on the crucial stretch that enabled the railway to break through the Rockies. At **Craigellachie**, right beside the road, about 25 km east of Shuswap Lake, a granite monolith marks the spot where the eastern and western sections linked up to form Canada's first transcontinental railway. At 9.22 a.m. on November 7, 1885, surrounded by top-hatted dignitaries and grimy overalled labourers, C.P.R. boss Donald Smith tucked in his flowing white beard and hammered home the famous Last Spike—after misjudging his first swing and bending a first spike double.

Leave the Trans-Canada 1½ km east of Revelstoke town to drive the winding **Summit Road** all the way up Mount Revelstoke, 6,300 ft, the only mountain in Canada that you can "climb" by car. This is the cosy way to watch the park's landscape change from dense lowland forest, through alpine meadows dotted with wild flowers, to the bleak tundra of the high country. From the top you look out over the Columbia and Illecillewaet river valleys and back to the Monashee Mountains. There are two campsites with

Keep your feet dry by negotiating the rapids on horseback—a delightful way to see the Rockies.

car access (not serviced) and several back country sites. Hikers wishing to camp off the highway need to purchase a back country permit, currently $2; this can be bought at 301 B Third Street. This is also the place to get your detailed maps and fishing permit. In the creeks and lakes, you'll find an abundance of trout—rainbow, brook, brown, cut-throat and red-spotted Dolly Varden—as well as whitefish, char and bass. Nature-lovers may spot elk, moose and mountain goat, bird-watchers look out for grey jay, blue grouse and golden eagle, while everyone should watch out for black bear.

Yoho National Park

From the railway depot and saw-mill town of Golden, the highway turns east to one of the prettiest of B.C.'s national parks, in the mountains and quiet lakes around the Yoho and Kicking Horse rivers. Buy your food supplies at the parkside town of Field and cut back to the signposted Emerald Lake turn-off. Just inside the woods is a pleasant picnic area beside the "**natural bridge**", a massive slab of rock through which the swift waters of the Kicking Horse River have forced a channel. A salt-lick just past the bridge often attracts moose at dawn and dusk.

Drive on up to **Emerald Lake,** a place of sheer magical peace, mirroring the mountains in its perfectly still green waters. With only one secluded, first-class but discreet hotel on its shores, the pear-shaped lake's tranquillity is less troubled by noisy tour groups than some of the more popular Rocky Mountain resorts. The path around the lake makes a delightful 2-hour ramble through woodland, giving you a good chance of spotting some of the park's small wildlife, notably some very chubby brown porcupine and an occasional beaver.

Back on the Trans-Canada at the turn-off to Field is the Park Information Centre. After 6 km

The Trans-Canada continues through the jagged mountains of **Glacier National Park**, which counts over 400 glaciers within its boundaries. **Rogers' Pass** was named after the major who found this corridor in 1882, thus enabling the C.P.R. to cut through the avalanche-prone Selkirk Mountains. It was also the toughest obstacle to clear for completion of the Trans-Canada Highway in 1962.

173

travelling east through the pine forests of the **Yoho Valley,** you will come to a turn-off for the spectacular **Takakkaw Falls,** where you will see the Kicking Horse Campground. Takakkaw is an Indian word for "magnificent", a fair description of the waters spilling out of the outflow of the Daly Glacier. Unlike many waterfalls, this one is at its most spectacular on the hottest summer afternoons, when the glacier ice melts. For a panoramic view of the glacier, take the Highline Trail 1 km south of the falls, starting out from the Whiskey Jack Hostel.

On the way back, stop south of the confluence of the Yoho and Kicking Horse rivers at a viewpoint for the **Spiral Tunnels.** Watch trains entering and reappearing from the upper of two tunnels bored into the mountain to form a figure 8. The lower spiral is visible from the Trans-Canada Highway. This engineering feat was necessary to overcome the steep gradient of the approach to **Kicking Horse Pass.** At the park's eastern exit, you'll see where geologist James Hector, member of an 1858 expedition mapping the major passes through the Rockies, was kicked senseless by a pack horse—whence the name of the pass. From Field, you can ride through the tunnels to Lake Louise.

Lake Louise

The fairytale setting of this blue, blue lake with its monumental railway hotel, **Château Lake Louise,** has made it the mecca of thousands of sightseers every year. The village (3 km east) is very much a tourist-trap, but the lake (named after a daughter of Queen Victoria) and its surroundings retain their magic. From the hotel terrace, before breakfast and the first crowds, look out onto the pine trees and snowy peaks of Fairview mountain to the south and the Beehive to the north, with the dazzling white Victoria glacier producing startling reflections on the shimmering surface of the lake. Give the mob the slip by walking along clearly marked paths to the far end of the lake, or walk the extra 2½ km to the teahouse. The path continues to the **Plain of Six Glaciers,** requiring more stamina.

Take the mountain road 14 km south to **Moraine Lake**—nice drive, wonderful all-day hike— to view the sawtooth skyline of the **Valley of the Ten Peaks** and the exhilarating climax of the lake's clear turquoise waters.

For a view of the whole area, take the cable-car from Lake Louise up **Mount Whitehorn.**

Explore the Rockies' glaciers in special panoramic-view ice-buggies.

174

Banff National Park

The first and most famous of Canada's national parks began, as so many things in this country, with the railways. When the C.P.R. reached Banff in 1883, the Rockies were suddenly opened up to public access, and the government decided, two years later, to preserve the region's beauty by declaring Banff a national park.

After three railway workers discovered hot sulphur springs bubbling from the earth, their bosses built one of their grandest castle-hotels, the **Banff Springs**, a monument to be visited even if you're not staying there. The turreted edifice set down in the Bow River Valley has something of the fairytale castles of Ludwig of Bavaria. Take a canoe out on the river. If you're feeling less energetic, take the waters at the **Cave and Basin Springs**, 3 km west of the hotel, or the **Upper Hot Springs**, a short drive south. The springs are 29°C in winter, rising to 42°C in summer. The cable-car from Upper Hot Springs up **Sulphur Mountain** will give you a panoramic view of the mountains around the Bow Valley.

One of many fine excursions is the drive along Bow Valley Parkway (Highway 1A), then a hike along the marked trail beside the rapids to the lower and upper waterfalls in **Johnston Canyon**.

Back on the Trans-Canada Highway towards Lake Louise, look out, to the east, for the crenellated silhouette of **Castle Mountain**, 9,390 ft high.

Icefields Parkway

This 233-km drive on Highway 93, up the spine of the mountain range from Lake Louise to Jasper, gives a rich sense of the Rockies' varied beauties—glaciers, waterfalls, lakes and canyons. Take a full day so that you have time to explore some of the sights on foot. Stop first at the **Crowfoot Glacier**, where you can see the foot's two remaining "toes", the third having broken away. The mass of ice facing you is 165 ft thick.

At Bow Summit, leave the Parkway at the signpost to the viewpoint overlooking the spectacular **Peyto Lake**, a deep turquoise colour at the height of summer. If you have time, stop at Kilometre 117 on the Parkway, to hike up the winding path to **Parker's Ridge** (6,560 ft) above pretty alpine meadows overlooking the Saskatchewan Glacier, the beginning of the great North Saskatchewan River that ends up in Hudson Bay.

Inside Jasper National Park, put on good rubber- or crepe-soled shoes to walk out onto the ice of **Athabaska Glacier**, part of the Columbia Icefield. You can also venture onto the ice sheet in a snowmobile. Note the rock debris or rubble (*moraine* in the language of glaciologists) in front of the glacier showing that the Athabaska is retreating—a hundred years ago it reached across to the other side of the Parkway.

Forget stock market crashes with a picnic down by Moraine Lake.

At the Parkway's 200-km mark, take Highway 93A to **Athabasca Falls**. A comfortable boardwalk leads you on an informative nature ramble right up to where the mighty river plunges over the narrow gorge.

The old fur trading post of **Jasper** is now a refreshingly peaceful resort town with a grand park lodge and fine facilities for rafting, canoeing, camp-

ing and other mountain sports. Take the cable-car ride up **Whistlers Mountain** for a view of the Rockies' highest peak, Mount Robson. One of the most attractive excursions is the drive along **Maligne Canyon**. Stop off to look down into the sheer limestone gorge at the roiling waters, sudden cascades and just as sudden tranquil pools. At the end of the canyon is **Maligne Lake** where the great attraction is a boat cruise around the picturesque Spirit Island.

ALBERTA

This province of ranches and oil derricks likes to cultivate the image of Canada's *Wild* West. If its politics are often conservative (opponents compare some of the leaders with the province's cherished collection of dinosaurs) they are of the adventurous brand favouring Calgary's rodeos and the commercial extravaganza of Edmonton's celebrated mammoth shopping mall.

With the discovery of huge oil fields after World War II, Alberta's economy boomed, the population exploded and confidence soared. The enthusiasm is dampened occasionally by downturns in world oil prices, but the atmosphere remains cheerful.

Alberta is very conscious of its geology. Alternating 600 to 200 million years ago between dry land and sea, the region developed a plant and animal life that decayed to form the oil, coal and natural gas at the base of the province's modern prosperity. Subsequent floods and earthquakes left the parched Badlands of the Red Deer River Valley as a protective crust, preserving the skeletons of the dinosaurs. They were discovered by surveyors looking for coal seams.

Calgary

In this part of the world, in past eras, gold rushes created cities out of a wasteland overnight and just as quickly returned them to dust. Soaring Middle East oil prices seemed to do the same thing for Calgary in the 1970s, but the shining downtown skyscrapers that shot up then do not look as if they are about to crumble. Not that Calgary was a wasteland when the post-World War II oil boom began, but it was little more than a cow town, better known for bronco-busting rodeos than business acumen. Population more than doubled from 280,000 in 1961 to 590,000 20 years later, chasing hard behind the provincial capital—and arch-rival—Edmonton.

Hotshot bankers have moved in to handle the new wealth, polishing up but not eclipsing the frontier image. While hand-tooled cowboy boots and Stetson hats are still popular, the business suits between the two are increasingly sophisticated, even Italian in cut, leaving the string ties and blue jeans for the Stampede.

The ten days of the **Calgary Stampede** in the first half of July are by any standards, anthropological or purely hedonistic, a phenomenon to be seen. Cowboy hyperbole demands that it be known as the "Greatest Outdoor Show on Earth", a title dating back to its beginnings in 1912. The Stampede was originally conceived to show all the techniques and excitement of rounding up cattle on the prairies. Today, at Stampede Park, it does indeed stage agricultural and garden exhibitions, displays of Indian crafts and dancing, and all the sideshows of a country fair.

But after the grand opening **parade** of baton-whirling majorettes, cowboys, costumed Indians, champion steers, and smiling stars of the chamber of commerce, the great attraction remains the **rodeo**. Bareback riding and bronco-busting, bull riding and steer-wrestling, calf-roping, wild horse contests and wild milking competitions culminate in the traditional **chuck-wagon races**. The Rangeland Derby, as it is known, races four-horse wagons like those used to bring food out to the cowboy on the range during roundup time. The

race begins with a tight figure-of-eight manoeuvre in the middle of the arena before the wagons suddenly break out onto the horse-racing track for a mad dash to the finish. The chuck-wagon races are said to have originated when the last crew back in town had to buy all the drinks—now the amount of prize money handed out totals over $200,000.

Just as much fun as the official events are the square dancing in the streets, the firework displays, the delicious barbecue dinners and the flapjack breakfasts.

Spend a more sober moment in the fascinating **Glenbow Museum**, 130 Ninth Avenue S.E. Beautifully arranged exhibits of furniture, costumes, utensils and weapons give a vivid picture of Alberta life, from the pioneers' log-cabin homesteads to the modern artefacts of oil-drillers, railway-builders and miners. The life of Ojibwa and Cree Indians is displayed in tepees, magnificent buffalo robes and beaded buckskin, dance masks and snowshoes.

The shops and offices of the downtown skyscrapers are linked by a network of all-weather bridges and subterranean galleries. One of the main shopping centres is the four-block **Stephen Avenue Mall**. For a view of the town's steel and glass urban canyons and the Rocky Mountains looming on the western horizon,

179

take the elevator to the observation deck of the 627-ft **Calgary Tower**. Immediately below it is a revolving restaurant.

Winter sports enthusiasts will appreciate the new facilities created for the 1988 Olympics. The **Canadian Airlines Saddledome** out at Stampede Park is equipped for ice hockey and figure-skating. A speed-skating rink has been installed in the **Olympic Oval** on the University of Calgary campus, which has gained attractive new student residences from the Athletes' Village. Off the Trans-Canada Highway, the **Canada Olympic Park** has built two ski-jumps and the country's first combined bobsleigh and luge run. Most popular with the tourists are the downhill runs at the **Nakiska** ski area on Mount Allan 80 km south-west on Highway 40, and the cross-country trails at **Canmore** (west on the Trans-Canada Highway) at the foot of Mount Rundle near the entrance to Banff National Park.

Drumheller

The area around this old coal-mining town is famous for the prehistoric fossils and remarkably complete remains of dinosaurs whose stamping grounds

Oil-prices rise and fall but Calgary still has the look of a boom-town.

were the **Badlands** of the Red Deer River Valley. The 130-km drive north-east of Calgary on Highway 9 takes you through wheat-growing country where you may see the farming communities of Hutterites, an austere religious sect originally from Slovakia, often persecuted for their pacifism. The women wear traditional dirndl costumes with headscarf and apron, while their husbands, dressed all in black with broad-rimmed hats, cultivate the heavy beards of Old Testament prophets.

Drumheller's **Dinosaur Trail** places fossils and lifesize models of the beasts in their original habitat—though you have to imagine a luxuriant humid jungle in place of the present-day arid desert. Looping 48 km round the Red Deer River, the trail starts out at Drumheller's **fossil museum**, 335 First Street, devoted mainly to the region's geology. But for a most exciting confrontation with the prehistoric world of dinosaurs, make for the new **Tyrrell Museum of Palaeontology** on the Midland provincial park's North Dinosaur Trail. This beautifully organized museum, drawing on the most modern audiovisual techniques, is named after Joseph Tyrrell, the geologist who made the first discovery of Alberta's 65-million-year-old dinosaurs while surveying coal seams along the Red

Deer River in 1884. Drawing on some of the finest of the 200 creatures unearthed in the area, the Tyrrell museum recreates jungle environments for superbly reconstructed skeletons and models, including Tyrrell's *Albertosaurus,* the awesome *Tyrannosaurus rex*, measuring 45 ft long and 19 ft tall in its cotton socks, and the "tiny" but most lovable of all, a duck-billed *Lambeosaurus,* just 10 ft tall, followed by her baby.

Edmonton

You can see the source of the provincial capital's wealth as you drive in from the airport. On the southern outskirts of town on Highway 2 are the derricks (some are reconstructions) and "grasshopper" pumps that have characterized Edmonton since the oil strike at the great well of Leduc No 1 in 1947. But the town has created another treasure trove in the astounding **West Edmonton Mall** (Stony Plain Road, 170 Street), a shopping centre to end all shopping centres, attracting as many as 80,000 customers on a busy day, 40 per cent of them from the United States. Why? What other shopping mall has: four submarines; a "waterpark" with 6-ft waves for surfing, sand-coloured rubber beach and 22 waterslides with frightening names like Howler, Sky Screamer and Corkscrew; 828 shops; 187

women's fashion stores; eight department stores; 110 restaurants; 5 nightclubs; aquariums and bird sanctuaries? It is to be hoped that the submarines will start offering champagne rides under the mall again on Saturday nights.

For a good view of the city, one used to be able to look down from the telephone building, but unfortunately this is no longer possible and there is currently no replacement observation tower.

SASKATCHEWAN

Even though revenues from oil, uranium, coal and natural gas now approach agricultural income, Saskatchewan is still known as "Canada's bread basket". During the Depression, it was the country's poorest province, close to starvation. But that all changed with the timely rise of local boy John Diefenbaker as the first federal prime minister from Saskatchewan. Farmers

On the Prairies, it's summertime and the fish are jumping.

won't ever forget the deals he got for their high-grade bread wheat in Russia and China. You can see the monuments right across the Prairies—gigantic cathedral-like grain elevators.

183

Regina

The queen Latinized in the provincial capital's name is, of course, Victoria. The city's decorum would please her. It's been cleaned up considerably since the first settlers arrived in the 1880s and found the banks of the Wascana Creek littered with hundreds of buffalo bones. Indian hunters used to dry their buffalo meat and stretch the hides by the creek, and would leave the bones in a heap. The town was known as Pile of Bones until they were ground up for fertilizer.

Today, you'll find the buffalo, along with other regional wildlife, prehistoric and present-day, in the **Royal Saskatchewan Museum,** on Albert Street. The museum is south of the city centre in the very pretty bird sanctuary **Wascana Park,** one of the few places in southern Saskatchewan where you'll see any trees. The creek has been dammed to form a lake; an information area is concentrated behind the **Saskatchewan Centre.** Also in the park is the provincial **Legislative Building,** with an interesting portrait gallery of Indian chiefs on the ground floor. On Lakeview Drive is the **Diefenbaker Homestead,** brought here from near Saskatoon to give a vivid insight into the simple country life led by Saskatchewan's most famous son before he went off to Ottawa.

Headquarters of the famous Mounties in the 1880s until moved to Ottawa, Regina keeps the **Royal Canadian Mounted Police College** as a major training centre (north of the airport at the end of 11th Avenue). Visit the barracks, crime laboratories and **museum,** which traces Mountie history from the first clashes with gold-rush panhandlers to wartime reconnaissance and latterday counter-espionnage. The old mess hall is now the "Little Chapel on the Square" where the stained-glass windows portray not saints but Mounties, notably a reveille bugler and guard in mourning.

At **Government House** (Dewdney Avenue, corner of Pasqua Street), you can see dramatizations of Louis Riel's treason trial.

MANITOBA

Flat the province may be, but it offers an astonishingly rich ethnic diversity in its rural and urban populations. In addition to Anglo-Saxon and French stock brought here by the fur trade, late 19th-century immigration campaigns have given Manitoba thriving communities of Ukrainian, German, Jewish, Polish, Dutch, Hungarian, Italian, even Icelandic origin, with more recent arrivals from Asia and the Philippines.

Winnipeg

Of the province's population, well over half (652,400) lives in its capital. In addition to the government bureaucracy, the town has a stalwart business community and proud cultural life, especially in modern art, ballet and classical music. Manitoba's many ethnic cultures provide the basis for its Folklorama festival which every August attracts some 40 pavilions featuring different national cuisines, folklore, craftwork and costumes.

The town's artistic and commercial worlds have joined forces in recent years to preserve the old business district's handsome turn-of-the-century architecture as a lively shopping and restaurant neighbourhood, north of Notre-Dame Avenue between Princess Street and Main Street. The **Old Market Square Warehouse District**, as it's now known, boasts many fine office buildings and warehouses inspired by the great Chicago School, including the Canadian West's first skyscraper, the 1903

Louis Riel, Rebel and Martyr

Was the founder of Manitoba a political hero or mad visionary? Few characters in Canadian history have excited more controversy than the French-Indian Métis leader, Louis Riel, born in 1844 on the Red River colony that was to become Winnipeg.

Riel studied theology and law in Montreal. He proved to be courageous and capable when he worked out feasible legislation for Manitoba's new status as a Canadian province in 1870. But his volatile personality cracked under the strains of armed conflict, American exile and finally imprisonment for his role in the execution of Ontario agitator Thomas Scott. In mental institutions in Quebec, Riel lapsed into moral decline and lost his sense of reality. He conceived

a religious mission to set up a New World Catholicism with the Bishop of Montreal as its Pope. He went back into U.S. exile, this time self-imposed, until 1884 when Métis farmers begged him to come and defend their legal rights in Saskatchewan. His armed rebellion of 1885, centring on the Métis stronghold of Batoche with a new "provisional government" like the one that had forced concessions from Ottawa 15 years earlier, collapsed within two months. At his trial for treason, the jury found him guilty, but recommended clemency. Despite conflicting expert arguments on his sanity, Riel was hanged in Regina, November 16, 1885, sparking the beginning of the nationalist movement. Métis and Québécois campaign to this day for a retroactive pardon.

Royal Tower (504 Main). On Old Market Square itself, on summer weekends, you'll find a colourful farmer's market alongside stalls of antique bric-a-brac and craftware.

Its vital stake in the grain and commodities market gives Winnipeg a strong financial as well as architectural affinity with Chicago, as you can see on a visit to the trading floor of the **Commodity Exchange**, open to the public at 360 Main (5th floor). This is just one of the town's many modern skyscrapers clustered around the commercial hub of **Portage and Main**, which has the reputation of being the windiest spot in Canada.

In the splendid **Manitoba Museum of Man and Nature** (190 Rupert Avenue), prehistoric and present-day animals are presented in beautifully recreated environments of Arctic wastelands, tundra, woodland and waterfalls, complete with bird sounds, eerie wolf howls or the terrifying roar of a forest fire. The province's ethnic groups are shown in traditional costume and old homesteads; special emphasis is given to Manitoba's Indians

and a Métis buffalo hunt. Be sure to walk around the reconstructed decks of the 17th-century **Nonsuch** ketch that pioneered Hudson Bay's involvement in the fur trade.

The museum adjoins the **Centennial Concert Hall,** home of the Winnipeg Symphony Orchestra, Manitoba Opera Association and Royal Winnipeg Ballet. If you're not around for the ballet performances there from October to May, look out for the summer Ballet in the Park shows in Assiniboine Park, west of town off the Trans-Canada Highway.

The **Winnipeg Art Gallery**, in a strikingly designed angular structure at 300 Memorial Boulevard, has an interesting permanent collection of modern Canadian and American artists, Inuit sculpture and usually first-rate seasonal exhibitions.

The old French-speaking community of **St-Boniface**, now a Winnipeg suburb, is on the east side of the Red River. It boasts on Avenue Taché the city's oldest building, the 1846 convent of the Grey Nuns. It's now the parish **museum**, devoted in part to the life of Louis Riel. Next door, you'll find his simple grave in the cemetery of St-Boniface basilica, completely rebuilt behind its white stone façade after a recent fire.

Children enjoy the 2-hour ride in the four wooden coaches and

When St-Boniface basilica burned down, only the façade survived.

187

caboose of the **Prairie Dog Central** steam train, from St. James Station to and from Grosse Isle, 25 km north-west of town. If you feel like a day at the beach, drive north-east on Highway 59 to **Lake Winnipeg**, where the most convenient swimming is at Grand Beach.

Churchill

This historic port offers a unique opportunity (with simple but comfortable hotel accommodation) to visit Hudson Bay. You can see beluga whales in summer, polar bears in the autumn and, if you're around at the spring or autumn equinox, the ''northern lights'' of the aurora borealis. The easiest way in is by plane, but if you want to see at ground level the Manitoba lakes and plains that fur traders crossed in the days of old, take the VIA train from Winnipeg, which leaves three days a week.

Even at the height of summer, take warm clothes for the brisk evenings. The little town has a true frontier atmosphere to it. The Hudson's Bay Company established a trading post here in 1717, and its store on the main street is still the place to get camping and hiking gear—or long underwear if a sudden blizzard blows up. Inuit craft shops offer not souvenir junk but genuine native handwork,

---

Polar Trip

Polar bears can be seen sailing lazily into Churchill harbour on ice floes that have travelled over 100 miles during the summer melt. More than 100 bears take this cruise as a change from the usual winter grind of hunting seal out on the ice of the frozen bay. On the southern shores of the Hudson Bay, they take it easy and switch to a vegetarian diet for a while—blueberries and green shrubs—though they won't say no to the odd duck or rabbit that comes their way.

Daddy Bear weighs half a ton, twice as much as Mummy. Very good athletes for their size, they'd beat most of us in a sprint, clear six feet at the high jump and are ace mountaineers on steep cliffs. They swim backstroke, with just their nose sticking out of the water. Mating takes place on the pack ice in April and May. After the autumn cruise, the mother moves inland to build an igloo-like maternity den burrowed into a snowbank, often a cosy two-bedroom affair. She gives birth around the New Year to a baby the size of a guinea-pig. After hibernation, they emerge in early spring to hunt for the tender new baby seals back out on the ice. After two years, when Baby Bear is big enough to look after itself, Mummy and Daddy set off on their Churchill vacation.

and leather and fur goods that do not infringe protected-species laws. The **Eskimo Museum** gives a good insight into Inuit life and art around Hudson Bay.

Wildlife tours around the bay and across the otherwise inaccessible hinterland are organized in giant-wheeled or half-track tundra buggies (half- and full-day excursions or overnight camping trips). This is your best chance of seeing the unique brightly coloured plantlife of the tundra—notably purple fireweed, wild orchids—blooming in August. In autumn, apart from whale and polar bear, ptarmigan and snowy owls, look out, too, for red and arctic fox, and lemmings.

Several **boat tours** explore the bay for close-up sightings of beluga whale and cruise over to the ruins of **Fort Prince of Wales** on a promontory at the mouth of the Churchill River. The Hudson's Bay Company's massive stone fortress surrendered to the French navigator La Pérouse in 1782, without firing a single shot.

If you want to explore on your own, rent a car and drive round the harbour and its monumental grain elevators on the way to **Cape Merry** for a good view of the fort, especially at sunset. Take your binoculars for the beluga whales that swim with the summer tide in and out of the river estuary.

THE NORTH

Every country needs its myth, and Canada's is the fabled North, the icy mystery in which it and the world like to cloak the national image. But there's a fascinating reality "North of 60", as locals call the territories above the 60° latitude, ignored until recently by everybody but the Inuit and Indians who live there, plus a few explorers and miners for gold and other valuables. Even today, if they ever staged a football game between the Yukon and the Northwest Territories, the whole population might just squeeze into the stadium.

But more and more adventurers from "the outside" head for the Yukon's rugged mountains or the Northwest Territories' eerily beautiful Arctic wastes (northernmost point just 500 miles from the Pole). In the old Klondike boom towns, people find a whiff of romance from the great gold rush of 1897. Lovers of the outdoors track the last free-roaming bison herds or fly in for the challenge of fishing the trout and grayling in Great Slave and Great Bear lakes. It's worth booking hotel rooms in advance.

Access by road takes several days, but there are plenty of regional airlines serving the north: Whitehorse; Yellowknife; and Iqaluit (for access, via Pangnirtung, to the Auyuittuq National Park on Baffin Island)—with charters to the interior.

THE YUKON

The Klondike gold rush did more than fire the western world's imagination with scores of novels, epic poems and films—it immediately opened up a whole vast territory with such mundane services as railways, roads, telephones, electricity and hot and cold running water. In a subarctic land of soaring mountains and elongated glacial lakes beside the great Yukon River, today's tourists can thank yesterday's prospectors for using part of their pay dirt for some creature comforts.

Close to the original action and still providing the most vivid testimony to the Klondike days, the boom town of Dawson City yielded in 1953 to the transportation and communications centre of Whitehorse as territorial capital.

Whitehorse

The town grew up as the terminus where prospectors transferred from the Skagway train to the Yukon River steamboats and is now the junction of the Alaska and Klondike highways.

Though a thoroughly modern town with a population of 22,200, the Yukon capital is proud of its **Old Log Church** on Elliot Street and some three-storey log cabins it calls "wooden skyscrapers". One of them houses the **MacBride Museum** (First Avenue), with a good collection of gold rush memorabilia and exhibits of Yukon wildlife.

You can visit one of the old sternwheel riverboats, the **S.S. Klondike**, moored at the end of Second Avenue. Upriver, 3 km south of town, take a 2-hour **cruise** through Miles Canyon on the *M.V. Schwatka*. At the **GuggieVille Goldpanning and R.V. Park** 3 minutes from Dawson City, you yourself can try panning for gold.

Dawson City

A day's drive from Whitehorse along the Klondike Highway, the old boom town counts 1,900 inhabitants today, but the national parks system has done a nice tongue-in-cheek job of reconstructing the monuments of its heyday. This is the place to be in the week of August 17, Discovery Day, for the Klondike River raft-

races, costumed street-parades, music and dancing. If you miss that, look out for the Outhouse-On-Wheels race at the beginning of September.

One of the town's summer attractions is **Diamond Tooth Gertie's Gambling Hall,** one of the country's few legal casinos, where red-gartered dancing girls kick it up to a honky-tonk piano. The gawdy **Palace Grand Theatre** is famous for its vaudeville, Gaslight Follies.

St. Paul's Church shows a good film on the Klondike days, while **Dawson City Museum** gives you all the inside information you need about gold-mining, displaying the prospectors'

At Diamond Tooth Gertie's, chances are your 12 will draw a 10 and bust.

tools and paraphernalia. Behind the museum is the log cabin of Robert Service, the diggers' lilting bard celebrated for *The Shooting of Dan McGrew* and *The Cremation of Sam McGee.* He himself avoided the tough life of the gold-miner for a cosy job at the local bank. And next door is the sod-roofed home of Jack London, who made more money from his novels of the wild North than the stake he worked on nearby Henderson Creek. Both literary shrines hold readings from the masters' works.

Kluane National Park

About 150 km west of White-horse on the Alaska Highway, the entrance to this beautiful wilderness reserve is at **Haines Junction**. The park's St. Elias Mountain Range offers a great challenge to climbers, including the highest peak in Canada, Mount Logan. You'll find moose and, in the remoter areas, timber wolves, black bear and grizzlies.

For safety's sake, check in at the park reception centre and get maps and detailed information on the hiking trails covering 240 km of challenging terrain. The vast Kluane icefield system is made up of more than 2,000 glaciers, and you can hike right to the rim of the spectacular Kaskawulsh Glacier from Kluane Lake on the eastern edge of the park. Bird-watchers spot eagles, falcons and hawks circling overhead. Fishermen come for the trout, grayling and lake salmon.

Hello, El Dorado

August 17 is Discovery Day in the Yukon, a territorial public holiday. On that day in 1896, George Carmack and his Indian brothers-in-law, Skookum Jim and Tagish Charlie, panned four dollars' worth of gold in a tributary of the Klondike River. As more and more of the yellow stuff turned up, Rabbit Creek was renamed Bonanza. Local miners swarmed into the area, but no word reached the outside world till some of the luckier ones sailed down the Pacific coast the following summer. The Seattle Post-Intelligencer reported "a ton of gold", and the rush was on for an estimated 100,000 fortune-hunters by the end of 1897. Before the White Pass & Yukon Railway was built, well-to-do prospectors went by steamboat, the poor struggled with pack mules across the Alaska mountains, and only the most foolhardy went the all-Canadian route across British Columbia or Alberta, taking two years to get there.

With its dance halls, cinemas, saloons, casinos and brothels for a transient population peaking at 40,000, Dawson City became overnight the largest town north of Seattle and west of Winnipeg and a lot more fun than either. To be on the safe side with so many Americans around, the Canadian government formally declared its right to the newly established Yukon Territory and sent in the Mounties to keep a semblance of law. By 1899, when the mob was drawn away by news of a strike in Nome, Alaska, an estimated $50 million had been spent on reaching and working the Klondike, roughly the same value as the gold that had been dug up there since George, Jim and Charlie made their strike.

NORTHWEST TERRITORIES

If you feel drawn by a rendezvous with the Midnight Sun, make for these immense lands covering one-third of Canada's total surface, where the tundra passes for lush meadowland compared to the icy expanses inside the Arctic Circle. The summer, when temperatures climb to a comfortable 21 °C in Mackenzie District (compared to − 30 °C in January), offers the blessed privilege of a dazzling explosion of wild flowers. Beluga whales come out to play around Baffin Island. From autumn to March, the magical northern lights of the aurora borealis are at their most brilliant.

Some of the locals up in the Arctic are a little long in the tooth.

Part of the fun of canoeing in the Northwest Territories is repelling all boarders.

Yellowknife

On the north shore of Great Slave Lake, the territorial capital is a modern industrial gold-mining centre serving as a convenient base from which campers and fishermen explore the interior. On June 21, when the sun just won't go down, the town proposes a golfer's (and caddy's) midsummer night's dream with the Midnight Golf Tournament. Even non-golfers pour in for the all-night parties and dancing in the streets. All through the summer, there is open-air theatre in **Petitot Park**.

To gain an insight into the lives of Arctic-dwelling Inuit and Dene Indians of the Mackenzie Valley, visit **Prince of Wales**

Wood Buffalo National Park

Straddling the Alberta border, this park presents a unique opportunity to see herds of the rare shaggy humpbacked wood buffalo or bison, 2,500 at last count, and plains buffalo in their natural habitat. You also have a good chance of spotting the endangered whooping crane. Park headquarters at **Fort Smith** (fly in from Yellowknife or from Edmonton) organize camping field trips and photo-safaris.

Auyuittuq National Park

Flights from Montreal or Ottawa take you up to Baffin Island and the world's only national park inside the Arctic Circle. Change planes at Iqaluit for the park entrance at **Pangnirtung.** In its lovely mountain setting on the Cumberland Sound, this peaceful Inuit town is an excellent place to buy Inuit carvings—and to start your viewing of harbour seals and beluga whales. Inside Auyuittuq, either by dogsleigh or on foot, you'll find plenty of opportunities to see the Arctic's summer flora and a fauna that includes the beautiful white fox and polar bears. Up on the park's **Penny Highlands,** ponder the thought that the ice on the Penny Ice Cap is a left-over from the last Ice Age that ended about 20,000 years ago.

Northern Heritage Centre. In the shops, the native art and craftwork are of particularly high (and authentic) quality, and reasonably priced.

Head over to the **Bush Pilot's Monument** for a good view of the whole town and the lake. Bush pilots will be your best help for getting out to some of the country's best trout-fishing on Great Bear Lake or other less accessible lakes.

WHAT TO DO

The problem in Canada is to decide what not to do. You'll have too many choices on your hands—what the French Canadians call an *embarras du choix*. The outdoors beckons with its endless sporting possibilities. The exuberance of the people offers a year-round celebration of the arts and folk traditions from the Old and New World. And a prosperous society puts its wide range of shopping facilities above and below ground—at your disposal whatever the weather.

SPORTS

Beyond the cities, the country is in some senses one big outdoor sports facility.

The first and most popular of Canadian sports is quite simply **camping**, quite a vigorous activity in itself and the basis for all the others. While commercial campgrounds offer the most modern conveniences, like hot showers and electrical appliances, particularly good for camping-cars and caravans, the national and provincial parks have simpler but more attractive sites near lakes and rivers, especially good for tenting off the beaten track.

Hiking takes you to the true heart of this country. But remember, the dizzy delight of

Parks—National and Provincial

To make the wilderness accessible to people without taming the soul out of it, Canada has done a great job of carving 31 national parks from its multitude of natural beauties. They range from the little bird sanctuary of Point Pelee at the southernmost tip of Ontario to the gigantic Wood Buffalo park (bigger than Switzerland) on the border of Alberta and the Northwest Territories. You can surf or just bask in the sun on the beaches of Vancouver Island's Pacific Rim, while others are dog-sleighing across the primeval ice of Baffin Island's Auyuittuq. These federally administered facilities are supplemented by over 1,200 provincial parks run by local government.

To get the best out of their amenities, write for information to The Canadian Parks & Wilderness Society, 160 Bloor St. E., Suite 1335, Toronto, Ontario, M4W 1B9. Park regulations are simple but firm: don't pick the flowers or cut trees for wood; hunting on park grounds is forbidden and fishing permitted only with a licence; no motorboats except where explicitly authorized. In any case, always spend a few minutes at the park reception centre to pick up maps, fishing licence, advice about campgrounds and the possibility of guides for nature tours or fishing expeditions.

leaving behind you the last vestiges of civilization is all the greater if you have a good pair of shoes. Flimsy tennis shoes won't do in the Rockies. Whatever the morning weather, pack something waterproof, a sweater for high altitudes or late afternoon, and a spare pair of socks. Major tip: take a small rather than big rucksack, if you don't want to end up carrying other people's stuff. Be sure to get detailed trail-maps from the park reception centres before setting off. If you want to graduate to **mountain climbing**, the best opportunities are in the Rockies and B.C.'s Coastal Range. But beginners may prefer the easier Laurentians, while veterans will head for the higher peaks in the Yukon's Kluane National Park.

Try **canoeing** on the rivers and lakes (incidentally, like the fur traders of old, a good way of transporting your equipment to remoter campgrounds). The Iroquois birchbark or Kwakiutl cedar dugout canoes have been replaced by canvas, aluminium, fibreglass or hardened rubber, but solid wooden canoes can still be rented at the parks. Unlike a little rowboat, where there's no great risk if you make a mistake, a canoe does require some skill and caution. Beginners start out on a quiet pond, and even long-time canoers stick close to the bank when venturing onto a river. For any prolonged expedition, go in a group with two or three canoes in case one capsizes. Experienced canoers like the challenge of the Inuit kayak. But if you want the thrills of shooting

Bugs and Bears

Luckily, the joys of camping compensate for its trials. St. Brendan, Newfoundland's first Irish visitor, wasn't kidding. Canadian mosquitoes really can seem the size of chickens, bigger the further north you go. Black flies are at their worst in June. Things get better in late summer, but try always to camp in airy open spaces. In any case, arm yourself with plenty of insect repellent—and lemon or orange peel to rub on your skin if your supply runs out.

Bears are a different kettle of fish. Don't feed them, even unintentionally, by leaving food scraps around the camp. Black, brown or grizzly, look at them from a respectful, downright reverential distance. Take your close-ups with a telephoto lens, and never use a flash. In bear territory, don't pad silently around like an Indian scout—make enough noise for them to know you're there. They don't like surprises. The worst mistake you can make is to think a sweet little cub won't hurt you. No, but his mother, maybe just out of sight, will tear you apart before you can say your first "ichi-kichi-koo".

197

the rapids without having to do the work, try **whitewater rafting**, a big group-sport on the Thompson River in B.C., the Ottawa River in Ontario and on the St. Lawrence's Lachine Rapids in Quebec. Waterproof clothing is usually provided, but it's a good idea to keep a change of clothing in the car.

Anglers are appropriately goggle-eyed at the abundance and variety of Canada's **fishing**, deep-sea and freshwater, in placid lakes and mountain torrents. Atlantic tuna, mackerel, cod and swordfish off the Maritimes, the matchless Pacific salmon (see p. 166) and sea bass on the B.C. coast; and in the myriad inland waters between the two oceans, trout of every imaginable species—rainbow, speckled, cut-throat, Dolly Varden—grayling, whitefish, pike and perch. Each province has its own licensing laws, so check about permits and restrictions with local tourist offices and park reception centres.

This is particularly important for **hunting**. The guides, often Indians, that can be provided for more remote fishing trips are frequently obligatory companions for hunters. Careful government-supervised wildlife control permits hunting of bear, moose,

Here's one B.C. fisherman who can go home and die happy.

wolf, deer, wild geese and other game birds, but no buffalo or polar bear—the latter being strictly reserved, in very limited numbers, for the Inuit and Indians—nor commercial fur-bearing animals like beaver or mink. If you prefer to hunt with binoculars or a camera, most parks are a paradise for **birdwatching**, some of the best sanctuaries being at Point Pelee (Ontario), Forillon (Gaspé, Quebec) and Yoho in the Rockies.

Horseback riding is very popular in the west and the Prairies, where novices can improve their technique on a ranch holiday. Leave bronco-busting to the cowboys. In Ontario, you'll see more riding caps and white breeches than Stetsons and blue jeans; for the fox hunt they even sport red coats. **Golf** and **tennis** are best away from the big towns, in country resorts like Montebello and La Malbaie, Quebec, around Georgian Bay and the Muskoka Lakes in Ontario, or outside Victoria on Vancouver Island. You can usually play at private golf clubs by showing your home golf club membership card.

Water Sports

Even a long way from the sea, facilities for water sports are first-rate. **Sailing** and **wind surfing** are excellent on Ontario's Georgian Bay, around the Thousand Islands or, more sedately, on the Rideau Canal and the smaller lakes of Quebec's Laurentians and Eastern Townships. Sailing becomes a veritable obsession on Nova Scotia's Atlantic coast and B.C.'s Horseshoe Bay. At best bracing in the park lakes and rivers, **swimming** is more relaxed in the warmer waters of the Pacific, especially on Vancouver Island's west coast— with a bonus of great waves for **surfing**. Prince Edward Island's almost balmy north coast is your best bet on the Atlantic. One of the great attractions on the Nova Scotia coast south of Halifax is **diving** for buried treasure among an estimated 2,000 wrecks.

Winter Sports

It's suggested that one of the most delightful winter sports is living in Canada in the first place. Among the others, **ice skating** is a national favourite, with rinks in practically every town, but it's even more fun out in the country, on the frozen lakes, rivers and canals. A popular rink sport imported from Scotland is **curling.** Try Inuit-style **ice fishing**, through a hole in the frozen lake. Around Emerald Lake, Banff, Lake Louise and Jasper in the Rockies, the **skiing**, cross-country and downhill, is world-class, reinforced by the 1988 Calgary Olympics. Quebec's Laurentian resorts specialize in torchlight night-skiing. **Snowshoe hiking** makes a welcome alternative for non-skiers, as well as **toboggan** and **dog-sleighing**. Québécois are great fans of the **snowmobile** (or ski-doo), for which club membership cards (day pass available for tourists) and a car-driver's licence are compulsory.

Spectator Sports

The undisputed king of spectator sports, indeed a national obsession from early autumn to late spring, is **ice hockey.** British soldiers garrisoned in Halifax, Nova Scotia, played a primitive form of this fast, brilliantly brutal game in the 1860s, but it was created in its modern form in 1879 by a student of Montreal's McGill University. The Montreal Canadiens team dominated the game for years with such legendary players as Maurice "Rocket" Richard and Bernie Geoffrion. Nowadays, it is the Toronto Maple Leafs, the Calgary Flames and the Vancouver Canuks who compete for first place. In late May, early June, you'll find restaurants and nightclubs mysteriously emptying as the people stay home to watch on TV the eliminating play-offs and finals of the game's supreme trophy, the Stanley Cup (donated in 1893 by governor general Lord Stanley). The National Hockey League includes American teams, but that doesn't

No point in rushing it when cross-country skiing through Touquin Valley in Jasper National Park.

upset people—all their best players are Canadians.

The counterpart to this is the fact that equally rough, tough **Canadian football**, almost indistinguishable from the American game, is completely dominated by American players. Without the same threat to life and limb (on the field), **soccer**—football as the rest of the world knows it—is a very poor relative.

In the summer, American **baseball** is big in Toronto and Montreal, while you can catch some **cricket**, naturally enough, in Victoria and Vancouver.

But all that is sissy stuff compared with **rodeo**, the great summer attraction not only at the Calgary Stampede, but all across Manitoba, Saskatchewan, Alberta and British Columbia. From a word meaning roundup, the rodeo demonstrates the skills necessary to the gathering of livestock for counting and branding. Events of bronco-busting, bull-riding, milking wild cows and chuckwagon racing follow each other at literally breakneck pace. In steer-wrestling, once known as bulldogging, a cowboy leaps from his galloping horse to bring down a running steer by seizing its horns and twisting it to the ground—fastest time wins. In the good old days, the "bull-dogger" rounded off the stunt by grabbing the steer's lower lip in his own teeth.

Annual prizes go to any foreigner explaining the difference between American and Canadian football.

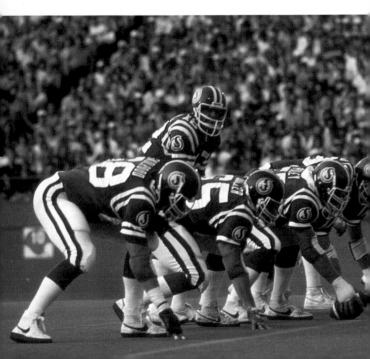

SHOPPING

They don't barter furs for blankets, copper kettles and whisky any more, but the commercial talents that founded this nation are still strong. The fortified trading posts on Hudson Bay, the Great Lakes and the St. Lawrence River have given way to giant shopping malls and subterranean labyrinths of boutiques, antique shops and even

whole department stores. With the harsh weather shut out, the countryside is brought indoors with streams, waterfalls, gardens or even a miniature pine forest. Just as the wily Scots of the Hudson's Bay Company tempted the Indians out of the woods to settle around the trading posts, so merchants of renovated historic neighbourhoods like Toronto's Hazelton Lanes entice shoppers into a maze of multilevel stores apparently designed to give them little hope of getting out again without buying something.

Canada's modern **shopping malls** are true microcosms of the world market, all over the country but nowhere more spectacularly than at the monumental West Edmonton Shopping Mall (see p. 182). In the big cities, most of the major French, Italian, American and Japanese designers of women's and men's fashions have either their own boutiques or special counters in the department stores. Designer clothes prices are comparable to those in the U.S., maybe slightly higher than in Europe, but remember to ask about reimbursement of provincial sales taxes for goods taken out of the country. One of the few bargains in an age when merchants seem to know the going world prices for everything is for Europeans shopping at **discount record stores**, most often located inside the malls. Watch the local newspapers for ads on special deals in the expanding compact disc market. Europeans should be careful when buying **electronic goods** such as stereo, video or computers to make sure they are compatible with the voltage at home.

The major **department stores** —Eatons and The Bay (Hudson's)—are highly competitive and closely comparable in quality. If you're looking for furs and leather goods, The Bay's centuries-old tradition gives it an edge. The company's blanket that won the hearts of the Indians is still a prestigious item.

All the major cities have some kind of **flea market**, usually at weekends in the renovated areas around the docklands. But many of the most enjoyable are out in the Great Lakes countryside of Ontario, the B.C. interior or Quebec's Eastern Townships. While paying for your picnic goods at a village grocery store, look out for the hand-written ads for **country auctions**. These are the occasions to pick up genuine antiques or old bric-a-brac not made in Hong Kong.

In this land of the great outdoors, hunting jackets and parkas are ruggedly efficient for dealing with the elements without attempting to be "fashionable", and particularly good in

Quebec and New Brunswick. In Alberta and B.C., look out for cowboy clothes—hand-tooled boots, belts and Stetson hats. In Newfoundland, you might want to invest in fishermen's oilskins and sou'wester hats in traditional yellow or elegant black.

After a long period of cheap mass production, Indian and Inuit craftwork is improving in quality with the native peoples' renewed pride and self-confidence. The best buys in clothes are Inuit mukluks (fur and sealskin boots), Indian moccasins, mittens and heavy-knit Cowichan sweaters (on the west coast). The Indians turn out fine basketry, beadwork, silver jewellery, black argillite and wood carvings, while the Inuit specialize in soapstone, onyx, bone and scrimshaw (etched ivory) sculpture. In Montreal, the Canadian Guild of Crafts (2025 Peel Street) has many samples of this work, while the Conseil des Arts du Québec (378 St. Paul West) can recommend shops for specific goods. In general, your best chance of finding high-quality craftwork is in museum shops, notably at Vancouver's Museum of Anthropology, Toronto's Royal Ontario Museum,

Adults are allowed into Vancouver's Kids Only Market—on condition they don't touch anything.

the McMichael Canadian Collection outside Toronto and the Glenbow in Calgary. And don't forget the craftwork of Canada's European cultures—quilts, rag dolls, rugs, needlework and ceramics, still to be found in country towns—and of Asia, in the oriental neighbourhoods of Vancouver and Toronto.

Collectors of **souvenir kitsch** will not be disappointed. In the concession shops at the filling-stations on the Trans-Canada Highway, you'll find some magnificent Royal Canadian Mounted Police dolls making peace with unsmiling wooden Indian chiefs (smiling chiefs are rarer and more expensive). Other serious junk includes rubber tomahawks, feather headdresses and, major item, acrylic beaver-tail fur hats.

FESTIVALS

Canada's brief but varied history is commemorated across the country with parades and street parties. Ethnic communities put on traditional costumes for annual pageants. Here is a far-from-exhaustive selection of folklore and cultural festivities:

January: *Vancouver* New Year's Day Polar Bear Swim in the ocean.

February: *Quebec City* Winter Carnival—ice-sculptures, pageant, canoe races, torchlight skiing. *Ottawa* Winterlude—ice and snow sculptures, concerts. *Vancouver* Chinese New Year (occasionally in January).

March/April: *Eastern Townships, Quebec* "Sugaring off" parties.

May: *Niagara Falls* Blossom Festival, *Ottawa* Canadian Tulip Festival—tulips, regatta, fireworks and beergardens. *Nationwide* (called Fête de Dollard in Quebec) Queen Victoria's birthday (May 24)—fireworks. *Niagara-on-the-Lake* Shaw Festival (until August).

June: *Stratford, Ontario* Shakespeare Festival (until October). *Charlottetown, Prince Edward Island* Summer Festival (until September). *Banff* Arts Festival (until September). *Montreal* Jazz Festival. *Yellowknife* Midnight Sun Golf Tournament (June 21). *Quebec* Fête Nationale—bonfires, parades, street dances (June 24). *Halifax* Nova Scotia Tattoo—Scottish pageant.

July: *Nationwide* Canada Day (July 1), *Ottawa* fireworks and variety show. *Montreal* Just-For-Laughs Festival *(Festival du Rire)*—international clowns and comedians in English and French. *Calgary* Stampede. *Edmonton* Klondike Days. *Saint John, New Brunswick* Loyalist City Festival—18th-century costumed pageant.

August: *Montreal* International Film Festival. *St. Ann's, Nova Scotia* Gaelic Mod—Scottish Highlands Festival. *Dawson City, Yukon* Discovery Day (August 17). *St. John's, Newfoundland* Regatta on Quidi Vidi Lake. *Winnipeg* Folklorama. *Regina* Buffalo Days—horse-racing, barbecues, brass bands and street dances.

September: *St. Catharines, Ontario* Grape and Wine Festival for Niagara Peninsula wineries.

October: *Kitchener* (formerly Berlin), *Ontario* Oktoberfest.

December: *Niagara Falls* Winter Festival of Light.

With the reassertion of ethnic pride, Indian and Inuit native handicraft has become a highly respected industry.

ENTERTAINMENT

After years of fighting an uphill battle against the competitive lures of the United States and Europe, Canada's performing arts are coming into their own with a new pride and enthusiasm.

Theatre in particular has staked out a place for itself on the North American scene with Ontario's prestigious Shakespeare Festival at Stratford and the Shaw Festival in Niagara-on-the-Lake. Your travel agent or Canada tourism office can help you book in advance for these highly popular summer events, which include light comedies and musicals along with the more serious fare. Toronto encourages contemporary Canadian drama at the St. Lawrence Centre for the Performing Arts and stages musical comedies at the Royal Alexandra Theatre and Bayview Playhouse.

French-Canadian drama is reviving in Montreal and at Quebec City's *Grand Théâtre*. But the great attractions in Quebec for French-speakers are its mordant **cabaret** artists and the comic or nostalgic **folk songs** in the *boîtes à chansons* (song clubs) that you'll find around Montreal's Rue St-Denis and along Quebec City's Grande Allée.

For **classical music**, Canada boasts two orchestras of international repute; the Montreal Symphony performs at the Place des Arts and the Toronto Symphony at Roy Thomson Hall. Meanwhile, the Vancouver, Winnipeg and Edmonton orchestras are growing in stature. When in Vieux Montréal, look out for the summer Mozart concerts in Notre-Dame basilica. Canada has always figured prominently in the world of **dance**. Among the most important are Toronto's National Ballet of Canada, Les Grands Ballets Canadiens of Montreal, the Royal Winnipeg Ballet and the Anna Wyman Dance Theatre of Vancouver. Performances of these companies, like the **opera** in Toronto, Ottawa and Montreal, are mainly in winter, but look out for occasional open-air summer shows in the city parks.

Jazz, modern and Dixieland, can be heard in the big cities' nightclub districts, but also during the arts festivals such as Montreal's, Stratford's and on boat-cruises like the Jazz-on-the-Lake ferries around the Toronto Islands. Major sports stadiums stage **rock concerts** in summer.

Nova Scotia's speciality is of course Scottish **bagpipe music** and **highland dancing** in Halifax and up on Cape Breton Island.

At the Nova Scotia Tattoo they still wear them just above the knee.

EATING OUT

Things are definitely getting better. It used to be said that, with all its divisive regional rivalries, one of the few areas in which Canada achieved unity, if not downright uniformity—with the possible and customary exception of Quebec—was in the kitchen. Now, a combination of greater affluence, more travel abroad, the influx of more exotic immigrants and regional pride in fresh local products has created a new generation of more discerning palates, for which foreign visitors can pronounce themselves well and truly grateful. From Pacific salmon to Atlantic lobster, Alberta beef and Yukon moose (don't laugh, moose steaks are succulent) to Ontario pheasant and Quebec

hams, proper justice is beginning to be done. And Italians, Russians, Chinese and Japanese are not ashamed of the Canadian company they keep.

Not that the old bland cooking of the Anglo-Saxons is any less dominant in the average middle-of-the-road restaurant here than it is south of the border. From one end of the Trans-Canada Highway to the other, you may find the same straightforward vegetable soups with a suspiciously familiar canned flavour, plain green salads, steak and potatoes, fruit pies and ice cream. But at last there are more inventive, spicier alternatives. And don't imagine that Quebec is an unquestionable gourmet's paradise. It does have good French restaurants, but it has a lot of bad imitations, too. Québécois cuisine is at its best a savoury version of the solid peasant cooking of western France, but it can be just as stodgy and monotonous as its old Anglo-Saxon counterpart. What counts in Montreal and Quebec City is the enduring Gallic habit of always demanding something better. It's a contagious attitude.

Canadian customs hold few mysteries for Americans, but may need some introduction for Europeans.

Breakfast. As soon as you sit down (any time from 7 to 11 a.m.), you're likely to see the waitress advancing on you armed with a pot of coffee. Serving coffee is the hospitable North American way of saying "good morning", and it takes firm, clear action to stop this auto-

Look across to Burrard Street Bridge while lunching on Vancouver's Granville Island.

matic gesture if you don't want coffee immediately. Hotel coffee is weak by European standards, but your cup will usually be refilled several times. In the big cities, espresso coffee addicts will find happiness at an Italian, Viennese or Hungarian café.

You generally have the choice of a "continental" breakfast of toast, croissants, doughnuts (*beignes* in Quebec) or muffins, with fruit juice and coffee, tea or hot chocolate; or American-British style, adding hot or cold cereals, waffles or pancakes with maple syrup, eggs and sausages or the great Canadian back bacon with very little fat. It's best of all as the lower layer of an eggs benedict on an "English muffin"—closer to an English crumpet—with poached egg and *sauce hollandaise*. In country and coastal villages, they may also serve fish and steak.

Lunch. On an active sightseeing day, follow the Canadian habit of a simple sandwich lunch (served from noon to 2.30 p.m.). A typical favourite is the submarine popular all over North America, the big, mouth-stretching sandwich of French bread stuffed with meatballs, sausages or ham, cheese, salami, onions, peppers, lettuce and tomatoes. No need for a dessert after one of these.

Dinner. The evening meal may begin earlier than in Europe,

around 6.30 or 7 p.m., though service continues to about 10.30. As in the U.S., cocktails are not necessarily considered apéritifs and may be served before, during or after the meal. If you prefer wine anyway, order it immediately and then everybody's happy. Similarly disconcerting to habitués of European cuisine, salad may be served before the main dish. Salad dressings are often surprising concoctions not familiar to every European palate. If you want a simple dressing, you can always ask for the oil, vinegar and a little mustard and mix your own *vinaigrette*.

Canadian dress habits are generally very relaxed, and it's only the dauntingly smartest restaurants that might expect men to wear a tie and women a dress or dressy slacks rather than jeans.

Regional Specialities

The new ecological awareness has reminded Canadians of the great natural riches they have not only in their national and provincial parks but also at their dinner tables. If you're travelling across the country, don't settle for the standard fare, seek out some of the local delicacies. From east to west:

Gourmets travel from all over the world to sample the lobster in the Maritimes.

The Atlantic Provinces. Nova Scotia, Prince Edward Island and New Brunswick are all justly proud of their lobster, best served at its simplest, boiled or roasted with a little lemon butter on the side, on the proper assumption that the meat is too good to be submerged in any fancy tomato or cream sauce. In this grand culinary rivalry, P.E.I. offers its Malpeque oysters, fresh, stewed or in a bisque soup. Nova Scotia counters with Digby scallops, fried, and clam chowder, a spicy soup with onions, potatoes and milk. New Brunswick proposes broiled salmon and shad amandine (with sliced almonds). Meanwhile, Newfoundland performs neat little miracles with its cod, using everything from the roe to the cheeks and tongue. P.E.I.'s potato pancakes turn its nickname of Spud Island into a royal honour.

Among some of the region's more exotic delicacies: New Brunswick's fiddlehead, a unique edible fern served steamed with roast lamb, and dulse, a chewable dried seaweed; Nova Scotia's solomon gundy, a delightful verbal distortion of salmagundi, a mixture of chopped meat and pickled herring in oil, vinegar, pepper and onions; and Newfoundland's nightmare for animal-lovers, seal-flipper pie.

P.E.I. produces the best local cheeses. For dessert, try the blueberry and rhubarb pies and fresh strawberries of Nova Scotia and New Brunswick. In Newfoundland, look out for the unique amber-coloured bakeapple berry, rich in vitamin C.

Quebec. Like frogs for the French, the province's heartwarming pea soup *(soupe aux pois)*, made with yellow peas and best when enriched with a ham hock, is famous enough to have served as a disparaging nickname for the Québécois themselves. A good onion soup *(soupe à l'oignon)* may be harder to find. With its roots in the peasant cuisine of their Normandy and Brittany ancestors, Québécois cooking makes no effort at sophistication. Pork and maple sugar are basic elements. Among the most common dishes, you'll find *cretons* (pork pâté), *andouillette aux fines herbes* (pork-tripe sausage) and *fèves au lard* (bacon-flavoured pork and beans). Maple syrup is used in curing ham, scrambled eggs, and in sauces for wild game, notably the fine partridge, grouse and Canada geese. Try to track down the great *tourtière*, a pie filled with venison, partridge or hare and finely chopped potatoes. *Cipaille* is a pie of game and potatoes separated by pie-crust into six layers.

More modest are typical snacks such as *poutine*, French

fries covered with melted cheese and barbecue sauce, and *guedille,* salad in a hot-dog bun.

Two of the country's best cheeses are the blue Ermite and Italian-style ricotta made by the Benedictine monks of St-Benoît-du-Lac in the Eastern Townships.

Not at all French, but an undoubted Montreal speciality, is the smoked meat sandwich—what London delicatessens call salt beef and Americans corned beef, served on rye bread with pickled cucumbers and cole slaw. They try to match it in Toronto and Vancouver, but refugees of the English-speaking diaspora that left Montreal in the 1970s still return on pilgrimages for the smoked meat on Boulevard St-Laurent.

Ontario. The province's countless lakes make freshwater fish the pride of the Ontario table: trout, whitefish and pike. The fish are baked in wines of the Niagara Peninsula. It's also great hunting country, and roast pheasant in maple syrup is a noted delicacy here. Around Niagara-on-the-Lake, the Loyalist tradition is upheld with a pumpkin pie that is naturally considered superior to anything produced south of the border.

Toronto's restaurant life has improved considerably with the assertion of its ethnic communities, particularly the Italians, Greeks, Chinese and, more recently, East Indian.

The Prairies. Wildfowl and corn-fed farm poultry are delicious in Manitoba and Saskatchewan, a good place to try roast turkey some other time than Christmas, served with red cabbage and a sauce of locally grown cranberries. Baked partridge and roast wild duck are superb. The corn on the cob makes a great lunch on its own.

Freshwater fish include baked lake trout and broiled pickerel, while Manitoba's caviar served with sour cream might impress many a gourmet Ayatollah or Commissar. From Lake Winnipeg comes the smoked goldeye and baked stuffed whitefish.

There comes a time when a man has to have a steak, and Alberta's beef is justly celebrated for the job, for plain old chuckwagon stew, too. Calgary's steak houses are excellent, but Europeans may be disconcerted at seeing steak and lobster occasionally served together. Barbecued chicken and ribs are a more successful combination. Buffalo steaks are uncommonly juicy, and rack of lamb and leg of pork are other ranch favourites.

Among desserts from the numerous wild berries, look out for the unique, slightly tart Saskatoon berry pie. A great breakfast favourite is hot biscuits with Dauphin honey.

British Columbia. The pride and joy of B.C. in general and Vancouver in particular is the Pacific salmon, freshly caught, superb whether baked or grilled, but always with no fuss. (A whole smoked salmon, specially packed for the journey, is a great gift to take home on your last day.) The shrimp, crab, black cod and halibut are among the best in North America. The freshness and variety of the seafood make the local Japanese restaurants a special attraction for some of the best sashimi and sushi outside Japan. By the same token, in Vancouver's wonderful Chinese restaurants, the best dishes are seafood.

The roast lamb, locally reared on Saltspring Island, is first class, though it's difficult to get the chef to prepare it with anything but mint sauce.

Gourmet hunters (the two often go together) insist that Canada's, nay, the world's best moose steaks, optimally cooked medium rare and served with a baked potato, come from the forests of the Yukon. But if you can't make it up there, you may hear of a local bag and cookout in the B.C. interior. Go: a once-in-a-lifetime experience.

The best of B.C.'s desserts are quite simply the Okanagan Valley's fresh peaches, apricots and apples (the latter, British-style with the local Armstrong cheddar cheese).

Sweet Maple

Maple sugar and syrup are uniquely North American products, with forests of the Maple Belt stretching from the American Middle West across to the Canadian Maritimes. Quebec accounts for 90% of Canadian production.

In the autumn, the maple concentrates its sugars in the "rays" or tubular cells under the bark. After maturing through the winter, the sugar sap begins to flow with the first warmer days of spring. Traditionally, holes are bored into the trunk to tap the flow through a pipe into a waiting bucket. Alternating freezing night temperatures and warmer days cause a pumping action that continues to produce buckets of sap for up to six weeks. The sap is boiled down in wood-fired vats and evaporated into syrup. About 150 litres of sap produce nearly 4 litres of maple syrup.

Modern industrial methods have replaced most of the old buckets with a more hygienic vacuum-tubing system to tap the sap right into the vats, but the buckets are still used as part of the ritual of the "sugaring-off" parties that celebrate the end of the long hard Quebec winter and the coming of spring.

There's more to Canadian dining than just beer and beef.

Drinks

Canada's national drink is beer—"it's all those lakes and rivers that make it so great"—served ice-cold, closer in strength and flavour to German or Belgian beer than the milder American. Cider, on the other hand, is much milder than the European brew.

Canada's two wineries, on Ontario's Niagara Peninsula and in B.C.'s Okanagan Valley, make not delicate, but quite respectable wines. The vines have to be tough to resist the cold, cold winters and occasional late May frosts. Grapes have to be imported from the U.S. to supplement Okanagan's production needs. French, Italian, German and American wines are easily available in big city restaurants, but the prices are high. A noteworthy exception is tax-free Alberta, so you can have a decent Bordeaux with that steak.

In Quebec, they'll pay the price. They'll also mix red wine with hard liquor and call it a *caribou*, a truly gut-warming cocktail for the long winter nights.

The connoisseur's drink here is Canadian rye whisky, best sipped, they say, neat and without ice.

BERLITZ-INFO

CONTENTS

A ACCOMMODATION

See also CAMPING. Many of the provincial tourist authorities inspect and grade accommodation annually. Official directories of establishments, available to the public free of charge, give full details of facilities and services.

Hotels. Many chains and individual hotels offer reduced rates on weekends, for families, for senior citizens, and during off-peak seasons. You can make nationwide reservations through the free booking services operated by most chains. Remember to specify your bed preference: single, double (a large bed for two), or twin (two beds).

A number of distinguished older hotels provide a high standard of personal attention in nostalgic surroundings. At low-priced hotels in small towns, you might not get a private bath or television.

Like their counterparts in the U.S., resort hotels offer special rates to guests who take their meals on the premises: A.P. (American Plan) includes three meals a day; M.A.P. (Modified American Plan), breakfast and lunch or dinner. On the European Plan (E.P.), no meals are provided—not even breakfast.

Motels, motor hotels and inns, usually situated near highways and main access roads in city centres and outlying areas, are a popular choice for tourists travelling by car. As a rule, motor hotels and inns are larger and have more elaborate facilities than motels. Many establishments have swimming pools and playgrounds.

Tourist or hospitality homes. Great for families and budget travellers, bed-and-breakfast accommodation—often a room or two with shared bath in a family home—allows you to meet Canadians while you save money.

Provincial and territorial tourist offices have addresses of local bed-and-breakfast associations, and some will make reservations for you.

Youth accommodation. For a complete list of hostels across Canada, contact the Canadian Hostelling Association, Suite 400, 205 Catherine Street, Ottawa, Ont. K2P 1C3; tel. (613) 237 7884. Non-members of the Hostelling Association can usually stay at a hostel if there is room, on payment of a small surcharge.

During the summer, some Canadian universities and colleges offer rooms in their residences. Tourist offices can provide addresses.

Alternatively, stay at the YMCA or YWCA, where you don't have to be a member to get in. Single or double rooms are the norm.

Camps and lodges. Camps and lodges are often located in remote areas and specialize in hunting or fishing, or naturalist activities such as watching wildlife and birds. Accommodation may be in cabins or cottages. Some have private bath and/or cooking facilities, while others have a separate building with dining-room and washing facilities.

Country vacations. Stay on a working farm or ranch and take part in seasonal activities—haymaking, lambing and the like—or simply relax in a rural setting. Some farms and ranches organize hunting and fishing trips, horse riding, hay rides, cross-country skiing, sleigh rides and other activities. Lodgings may be with the farm or ranch family, or in separate accommodation on the grounds. Where meals are not provided, they are usually available on request. Don't miss the chance to sample farm-fresh produce, home-raised beef, lamb and poultry, and home-baked bread, pancakes and berry pie.

AIRPORT INFORMATION

Calgary. *Calgary International*, 18 km outside the city centre. Airport buses circulate frequently between town and airport, stopping at the major hotels en route. Taxis are always on hand for the trip into Calgary. A coach service operates from the airport to Banff and Lake Louise.

Halifax. *Halifax International*, 42 km from the city. Take a taxi to the centre or catch the airport bus, which goes to major downtown hotels. Departures are frequent.

Montreal. *Mirabel airport* (55 km) handles chiefly intercontinental flights, while *Dorval airport* (23 km) handles mainly North American flights. Airport buses travel between the two airports, from Dorval to major downtown hotels, and from Mirabel to the centre. Taxis are also available, as are local buses from Dorval that connect with the subway.

Edmonton. *Edmonton International*, 29 km. "Airporter" van leaves frequently from major downtown hotels. There is also service from other parts of the city, including the West Edmonton Mall. No city buses serve the airport.

Ottawa. *Ottawa International,* 18 km. Airport buses run frequently to downtown hotels.

Toronto. *Lester B. Pearson International,* 30 km. In addition to the airport bus to the centre, Pacific Western buses run between the airport and Islington, Yorkdale and York Mills underground (subway) stations. Alternatively, you can take a limousine or taxi into town.

Vancouver. *Vancouver International*, 18 km. "Airporter" buses go to the central bus station, making stops at major hotels along the way. Vancouver city buses serve the airport but it is necessary, as well as inconvenient, to make one transfer to get to the centre. There are plenty of taxis.

Porter!	**Porteur!**
Where's the bus for...?	**Où est l'autobus pour...?**

ALCOHOL REGULATIONS

Laws regulating the sale and consumption of alcohol vary from province to province. The legal drinking age is 18 in Alberta, Manitoba and Quebec, and 19 elsewhere. The purchase of alcohol is restricted to certain hours and days in some places and prohibited altogether in others. Licensed restaurants serve beer, wine and spirits.

In most provinces, beer, wine and spirits are available exclusively at licensed liquor stores (closed Sundays and holidays), or beer vendors. It is against the law to carry open bottles of beer, wine or spirits inside a car.

C CAMPING

There's nothing like a holiday in Canada's great outdoors—whether you rough it in the Rockies or explore the tranquil shores of Ontario's lakeland. The number of campsites runs well into the thousands, including national, provincial, municipal and privately run campgrounds in parks, cities and towns. A network of sites spans the length of major highways including the Trans-Canada, with many campgrounds situated both on well-travelled routes and in more remote areas. In addition to toilets, showers and hook-ups for RVs (Recreational Vehicles, or campers), laundry, cooking and sports facilities may be provided. Off the beaten path, campgrounds typically consist of a cleared area for tents with toilets or privies, picnic tables and grills.

A few words of warning:

● Outside urban areas, insects can be voracious in late spring and summer. Have repellent on hand, as well as netting for tents and screens for RVs.

● In many areas, temperatures can plummet at night, even in summer. Be sure you have enough bedding and warm clothing.

● People can and do get lost in Canada's vast open spaces. If you're heading for a back country destination, be sure to notify someone of your whereabouts and expected time of return. That way, they can send out a search party if you fail to show up.

● Don't approach wild animals or attempt to feed them. And don't leave provisions lying about. Bears in particular may be attracted by food—or garbage. Dispose of remains in designated areas only.

May we camp here, please?	**Pouvons-nous camper ici, s'il vous plaît?**
We have a tent/a trailer	**Nous avons une tente/une caravane.**

CAR HIRE

Cars and campers (RVs) may be hired at major airports (24-hour service) and sea ports and in many towns and cities. Numerous local firms vie with the well-known international companies, keeping prices competitive. It's a good idea to book well in advance for the peak tourist period. Always ask about special offers and package arrangements, including reasonable weekend or monthly rates. It's also advisable to take comprehensive rather than third-party insurance. Look in the *Yellow Pages* under "Automobile Renting" for a complete listing of car hire agencies.

Payment is usually by credit card. Otherwise, the customer is required to make a substantial cash deposit. Some firms may refuse to rent cars if the customer does not have a credit card. Some firms set the minimum age at 21, others at 25.

A surcharge may be made if you hire a car in one city and leave it in another. A vehicle hired in the U.S. for use in Canada must be accompanied by a contract to that effect.

CLIMATE AND CLOTHING

Canada's climate varies tremendously with the season and the latitude—from the temperate south to the ice-bound Arctic Circle. Summers are short but hot over much of the country, with milder, rainier weather year-round on the Pacific coast. So bring plenty of cool cottons, plus lightweight woollens and a raincoat for a visit to British Columbia.

The far north warms up surprisingly during the summer months, though you may feel cold at night and in the early morning if you're hunting, fishing or camping out. Dress in layers you can shed when the sun comes up.

Winters are severe almost everywhere. To ward off the chill, you'll need a heavy overcoat, as well as snow boots, hat, scarf and gloves. And don't forget clothes for winter sports—skiing, snow-mobiling and sleighing.

Canadians tend to dress casually, even in the evening. At restaurants in the better resorts, most men wear a jacket at night, if not a tie, and a jacket and tie at smart restaurants in the big cities.

Monthly average maximum and minimum daytime temperatures in degrees Fahrenheit:

		J	F	M	A	M	J	J	A	S	O	N	D
Halifax	max.	32	31	38	47	59	68	74	74	67	57	46	35
	min.	15	15	23	31	40	48	55	56	50	41	32	21
Toronto	max.	30	31	40	53	64	75	80	78	71	60	46	34
	min.	18	19	27	38	47	57	62	61	54	45	35	23
Quebec City	max.	18	21	32	46	63	72	77	73	64	52	37	23
	min.	1	3	16	28	41	50	55	54	45	36	25	9
Edmonton	max.	5	14	16	39	52	60	62	61	52	43	25	14
	min.	-2	7	3	30	41	50	54	52	43	32	18	5
Vancouver	max.	41	44	50	58	64	69	74	73	65	57	48	43
	min.	32	34	37	40	46	52	54	54	49	44	39	35

And in degrees Celsius:

		J	F	M	A	M	J	J	A	S	O	N	D
Halifax	max.	0	-1	3	8	15	20	23	23	19	14	8	2
	min.	-9	-9	-5	-1	4	9	13	13	10	5	0	-6
Toronto	max.	-1	-3	4	12	18	24	27	26	22	15	8	1
	min.	-8	-7	-3	3	8	14	16	16	12	7	2	-4
Quebec City	max.	-8	-6	0	8	17	22	25	23	18	11	3	-5
	min.	-17	-16	-9	-2	5	10	13	12	7	2	-4	-13
Edmonton	max.	-15	-10	-9	4	11	15	17	16	11	6	-4	-10
	min.	-19	-14	-16	-1	5	10	12	11	6	0	-8	-15
Vancouver	max.	5	7	10	14	18	21	23	23	18	14	9	6
	min.	0	1	3	4	8	11	12	12	9	7	4	2

COMMUNICATIONS

Post offices. The Canadian postal service deals only with mail. Hours at major post offices are generally from 8 a.m. to 5.45 p.m., Monday to Friday. Some are also open either half a day or all day Saturday. Stamps are sold at post offices, at hotels, drugstores and other small shops displaying a Canada Post emblem. Often, postal franchises in drugstores and small businesses have longer working hours. Mail boxes are red.

General delivery (poste restante). You can have mail marked "General Delivery" sent to you care of the main post office of any town. Letters should carry a return address and the words "Hold for 15 days" (mail will not be kept longer).

Telegrams. This service is operated by Unitel Communications and various private companies (see yellow pages).

Telepost. Messages transmitted to any Unitel Communications office will be delivered by post to addresses in Canada or the U.S. the next day or sooner.

Telephone. The system is private, integrated with that of the United States. Long-distance and international calls can almost always be dialled direct from hotel rooms, though surcharges may be high. If you want to make a personal or a collect call, ask the operator to place it for you. Calls can be charged to a U.S. telephone credit card.

Dial 1 before the area code for long-distance calls, and 1 before the number for long-distance calls within the same area. Dial 0 for the operator, and for information on local numbers dial either 411 or 1 555-1212 (no charge).

COMPLAINTS

Managers of shops, hotels and restaurants are nearly always available to assist you if you have a complaint. Otherwise, contact the nearest tourist information agency for advice. Taxi companies will usually take up complaints about drivers, but you should know the driver's name and identification number (on display in the cab).

CRIME AND THEFT

Incidents of urban violence and street crime are rare. People walk about comfortably after dark in the town centres, looking in the shop windows and dropping in to the cafés and restaurants. Nevertheless, it's always a good idea to take a few precautions. Avoid badly lit or run-down areas at night. Store any valuables and reserves of cash in the hotel safe. Be sure to lock your car and hotel room. Keep a photocopy of your plane tickets and other personal documents, with a note of the phone and telex numbers of your travel agent: they could come in useful in case of loss or theft.

CUSTOMS AND ENTRY REGULATIONS

U.S. citizens must have some type of identification and proof of address (voter registration card, birth certificate or passport) to present to the Canadian officials when entering and the U.S. authorities when returning home. A driving licence is not accepted as identification. British subjects and citizens of most European and Commonwealth countries, including Australia and New Zealand, need only a valid passport—no visa—to enter Canada. But you could be asked at customs to show a return ticket and to prove that you have enough money for each day of your stay.

The following chart lists the main duty-free items you may take into Canada and, when returning home, into your own country:

Into:	Cigarettes	Cigars	Tobacco	Spirits	Wine
Canada	200 and	50 and	1 kg.	1.1 l. or	1.1 l.
Australia	200 or	250 g. or	250 g.	1 l. or	1 l.
Eire	200 or	50 or	250 g.	1 l. and	2 l.
N. Zealand	200 or	50 or	250 g.	1.1 l. and	4.5 l.
S. Africa	400 and	50 and	250 g.	1 l. and	2 l.
U.K.	200 or	50 or	250 g.	1 l. and	2 l.
U.S.	200 and	100 and	*	1 l. or	1 l.
*A reasonable quantity					

There's no limit to the amount of currency that can be imported or exported without declaration.

I've nothing to declare.	**Je n'ai rien à déclarer.**
It's for personal use.	**C'est pour mon usage personnel.**

D DRIVING

Crossing the border. Cars registered in the United States may be brought into Canada by the owner or his authorized driver for the duration of its registration period. The necessary formalities can be taken care of at the border.

U.S. visitors taking a car into Canada will need:

- A valid U.S. driver's licence
- Car registration papers
- Interprovince Motor Vehicle Liability
- Insurance Card or evidence of sufficient insurance coverage to conform with local laws (available from an insurance agent).

An international driving permit is highly recommended for visitors from non-English-speaking countries.

Breakdowns. If you have a breakdown, pull over onto the shoulder, raise the bonnet (hood) and wait for help—or walk to the nearest roadside emergency telephone (NB this could be 50 miles away).

The Canadian Automobile Association (C.A.A.) provides members and international affiliates with some breakdown assistance and travel information (itineraries, maps, guide books), as well as the services of an accommodation reservations desk and travel agency. For further information contact the Canadian Automobile Association:

2525 Carling Ave., Ottawa, Ontario, K2B 7Z2; tel. (613) 820-1890.

On the road. Regulations are similar to those in the U.S.: drive on the right, pass on the left, yield right of way to vehicles coming from your right at unmarked intersections. Traffic signs display the standard international pictographs. Speed limits are given in kilometres. Maximum speed on most highways and expressways is 100 kph (60 mph), on other roads 80 kph (50 mph), in towns 50 kph (30 mph), and near schools and parks 30 kph (20 mph). The use of seat belts is obligatory in all of Canada.

It is illegal to drive while under the influence of alcohol. If you surpass the acceptable limit you risk a stiff fine, imprisonment—or both.

Fuel is sold by the litre. Diesel, propane and three unleaded grades of gasoline are available. Leaded fuel is no longer sold. Always top up the tank before setting off into sparsely populated areas. Stations in many towns close at 7 p.m. weekdays and all day Sunday; those on the motorways often provide 24-hour service. Most filling stations offer both service and self-service.

Road signs are usually either in French or English, or are self-explanatory symbols. If you do, however, find yourself in an exclusively French-speaking area, here are the most common written ones:

Arrêt	*Stop*
Attention	*Caution*
Cédez	*Yield, give way*
Défense de stationner	*No parking*
Ecole/Ecoliers	*School/Schoolchildren*
Lentement	*Slow*
Piétons	*Pedestrians*
Réparations	*Road works*
Sortie de camions	*Lorry (truck) exit*
Stationnement	*Parking*
Are we on the road to...?	**Sommes-nous sur la route de...?**
Fill the tank, please.	**Faites le plein, s'il vous plaît.**
Check the oil/tyres/battery.	**Vérifiez l'huile/les pneus/ la batterie.**
My car has broken down.	**Ma voiture est en panne.**

DRUGS

The possession and use of drugs is strictly against the law in Canada. Customs officials are ever on the lookout for offenders, and no holiday-maker caught with illegal drugs, hard or soft, is likely to get off lightly.

E ELECTRIC CURRENT

The current is the same as in the U.S.: 110–120 volt, 60-cycle AC. Plugs are the standard two-flat-prong American type, so European visitors should buy a plug adaptor before they leave for Canada if they bring in electrical appliances.

EMBASSIES AND CONSULATES

The embassies listed below are all to be found in Ottawa, Canada's capital.

Australia:	High Commission, Suite 710, 50 O'Connor, Ottawa, Ont. K1P 6L2; tel. (613) 236-0841
Eire:	Embassy of Ireland, Suite 1105, 130 Albert St., Ottawa, Ont. K1P 5G4; tel. (613) 233-6281/2
Great Britain:	High Commission, 80 Elgin St., Ottawa, Ont. K1P 5K7; tel. (613) 237-1530
New Zealand:	High Commission, Metropolitan House, Suite 727-99 Bank St., Ottawa, Ont. K1P 6G3; tel. (613) 238-5991

| **South Africa:** | High Commission, 15 Sussex Drive, Ottawa, Ont. K1M 1M8; tel. (613) 744-0330 |
| **U.S.A.:** | Embassy, 100 Wellington St., Ottawa, Ont. K1P 5T1; tel. (613) 238-4470 |

Australia, South Africa and the U.S.A. maintain consulates in the big cities. You can obtain the addresses and telephone numbers from your embassy.

EMERGENCIES
In the big cities, dial 911 for emergency calls to the police, fire department or ambulance service. Elsewhere, dial 0 for the operator, who will transmit your SOS to the appropriate emergency service.

In summer, urgent messages can be sent to travellers in Canada via the "Tourist Alert" programme operated in conjunction with the Royal Canadian Mounted Police.

FISHING AND HUNTING REGULATIONS   F
To fish in Canada's lakes and rivers, non-residents must have a permit, issued by the various provincial governments and valid only within the province of issue. Permits are normally available at sporting goods stores, fishing camps, and marinas. Separate licences might be required for certain species of fish. In British Columbia, a separate licence is required for fishing in offshore waters. Contact the Department of Fisheries and Oceans:

Suite 400, 555 West Hastings St., Vancouver, B.C., V6B 5G3; tel. (604) 666-6331.

Anglers in national parks require a separate licence, available from Parks Canada offices, which is valid in all national parks where fishing is permitted.

The provinces also control hunting permits, except for the federal migratory game bird licence. Apply for the latter at any post office. Non-resident sportsmen may be required to hire an official guide.

Open seasons, bag limits and other restrictions vary according to province, so check with the authorities in the area you plan to visit. The tourist information office will put you in touch with the appropriate agency.

G GETTING TO CANADA

By Air. Air service is available from most major European cities to one or more of the following Canadian gateway cities—Halifax, Montreal, Toronto, Calgary, Edmonton and Vancouver.

Frequent flights connect the major U.S. cities to centres across Canada. Flying time from London to Toronto is 7½ hours, from New York 1½ hours. The journey from London to Vancouver takes 9½ hours (7 hours from New York).

Travel operators feature many charter flights and package tours, including city stays, camping holidays, adventure tours and northern expeditions. Hotel accommodation and car/RV hire may also be included.

Travellers from Australia, New Zealand and South Africa can visit Canada on an overall tour of North America.

By Rail. Amtrak and other U.S. companies link up with VIA Rail in eastern Canada. There is a service to Montreal from New York City and to Toronto via Buffalo. On the west coast of the U.S., train travellers must take a bus from Seattle to connect with VIA Rail in Vancouver. The Canrailpass, good for unlimited rail travel for a specific period, can be purchased either in Canada or before you leave home.

By Coach. Coach travel may not always be the most economical way to get around; often, the plane works out cheaper. Any Greyhound office can give you details of the many different routes and fares available to Canada. Ameripass tickets are valid for the following routes into Canada: Seattle to Vancouver; Grand Forks to Winnipeg; Buffalo and Detroit to Toronto.

By Sea. Marine Atlantic ferries carry cars and passengers between Bar Harbour, Marine and Yarmouth, Nova Scotia—a journey of some six hours. On the west coast, boats run between Seattle and Victoria. It's a good idea to reserve passage well in advance for peak periods.

By Road. Travel from the United States to Montreal is via U.S. Highway 87, 89 or 91. If you're heading for Toronto, follow Queen Elizabeth Way from Niagara Falls, or Highway 401 (Macdonald-Cartier Freeway) from Detroit. U.S. Interstate 5 leads to Seattle and the Canadian border. From there, it's just half-an-hour's drive into Vancouver on Canadian Highway 99.

HEALTH AND MEDICAL CARE

Large hotels will have a contact number for a doctor or nurse. You can also seek treatment for minor complaints at medical centres in many cities. Hospital care is of a very high standard, and emergency rooms generally give swift and efficient service. But medical fees can be costly, so make sure your health insurance will cover you while in Canada.

Don't let insect bites or sunburn spoil your holiday. Mosquitoes and black flies proliferate in summer, especially in woodlands and around lakes, and the Canadian sun can be very fierce. Insect repellent and sun-screen lotions are easily available.

I need a doctor/dentist.	**Il me faut un médecin/dentiste.**

LANGUAGE

French and English are the two official languages. Canadian English largely resembles American English. In Quebec, Canada's Francophone province, people appreciate your attempts to speak French, even if it's a simple "Bonjour" or "Merci". Canadian French differs from French French just as American English is different from British English—see p. 85 for a few hints. The Berlitz FRENCH PHRASEBOOK AND DICTIONARY covers most situations you're likely to encounter in Quebec. And the following expressions may come in useful:

Do you speak English?	**Parlez-vous anglais?**
Good morning/Good day	**Bonjour**
Please	**S'il vous plaît**
Thank you	**Merci**
You're welcome	**Bienvenue**
What does this mean?	**Que signifie ceci?**
I don't understand.	**Je ne comprends pas.**
Please write it down.	**Veuillez bien me l'écrire.**
yes/no	**oui/non**
left/right	**gauche/droite**
up/down	**en haut/en bas**
good/bad	**bon/mauvais**
big/small	**grand/petit**
cheap/expensive	**bon marché/cher**
hot/cold	**chaud/froid**
old/new	**vieux/neuf**
open/closed	**ouvert/fermé**

M MAPS

The provincial tourist authorities distribute excellent free maps. Canadian Automobile Association (C.A.A.) maps and town plans are available to members and affiliates without charge. The Canada map office sells both general maps and detailed topographic maps for hikers. Write to the Canada Map Office:

Department of Energy, Mines and Resources, 130 Bentley Avenue, Ottawa, Ontario K1A 0E9; tel.: (613) 952-7000.

The maps in this book were prepared by Falk-Verlag, Hamburg.

I'd like a street plan of...	**J'aimerais un plan de...**
a road map of this region	**une carte routière de cette région**

MONEY MATTERS

Currency. The Canadian dollar is printed in both English and French; each denomination is a different colour.

Coins: 1, 5, 10 and 25 cents and 1 dollar (known as the "looney"). In 1996 a $2 coin will come into circulation.

Bills: 2, 5, 10, 20, 50, 100 and 1,000 dollars.

The Canadian coin names are similar to the American: penny, nickel, dime, quarter, half-dollar, looney. In French, the are *sou, cinq sous, dix sous, vingt-cinq sous, cinquante sous* and *piastre*.

For currency restrictions, see CUSTOMS AND ENTRY REGULATIONS.

Currency exchange. Standard banking hours are 9.30 or 10 a.m. to 3 p.m. Monday to Wednesday; later on Thursdays and Fridays.

Banks offer the best exchange rate, no matter what the currency, though some of them might refuse to change U.S. bills of large denominations. Almost all hotels will change U.S. currency and traveller's cheques. Currency exchange offices at border crossing points also change money at the official rate.

Credit cards. The major international credit cards are accepted everywhere in Canada. In fact, you'll be at a disadvantage if you travel without a card: hotels and motels may ask you to pay for your room in advance, and car hire firms will invariably require you to make a sizable cash deposit.

Traveller's cheques. You'll have no problem cashing the well-known cheques issued in Canadian or U.S. dollars. Always carry your passport or driver's licence for identification.

Sales tax. Depending on the province, a sales tax of up to 12% is added to the purchase price of most goods, including hotel and restaurant bills in some cases. The Northwest Territories and Yukon have no sales tax, and Alberta's sales tax of 5% applies only to accommodation. In addition to provincial sales tax, a 7% federal sales tax (GST) applies to all goods and services bought in Canada. Visitors can claim a partial rebate of this tax by acquiring the relevant form at customs on leaving Canada.

Tax refunds. If you post or ship home purchases over a stipulated amount, you might not be charged any sales tax. In some provinces, visitors are eligible for a total or partial rebate provided they complete the relevant form. Ask at the tourist office for details.

POLICE

The R.C.M.P. (Royal Canadian Mounted Police) is Canada's federal police force. At ceremonial functions, "Mounties" can be recognized by their distinctive red serge jackets and wide-brimmed hats. In addition to their federal duties, R.C.M.P. officers are normally assigned to small towns, rural areas, and highway patrol across most of Canada, while municipal police forces operate in cities.

Where's the nearest police station?	**Où se trouve le poste de police le plus proche?**

PRICES

To give you an idea of what to expect, here's a sampling of average prices in Canadian dollars. They can only be approximate, however, owing to inflation and regional differences in the cost of living. Note that prices quoted in Canada do not as a rule include sales tax or GST.

Accommodation (double room per night). Hotels: luxury $180–325, moderate $55–120. Motels $45–200.

Cigarettes. Canadian $3.20 for 25, U.S. $2.50 for 20.

Entertainment. Nightclub/discotheque $5 and up, cinema $5.50 and up, theatre, opera and ballet $20 and up.

Hairdressers. *Man's* haircut (barbershop) from $15. *Woman's* cut from $20, shampoo and blow-dry $15 and up, permanent wave $35–100.

Meals and drinks. Breakfast from $4, snack bar lunch from $5, restaurant meal $15-50, coffee/soft drinks $1.50, cappuccino $2.25-3, bottle of wine from $16, beer $3-5, cocktails from $5.

Public transport. Subway, bus, streetcar $1.80 and up. Series of tickets and monthly pass available at lower rates.

Taxis. Drop rate $2.25, plus $1 per kilometre on average.

PUBLIC HOLIDAYS

When a holiday falls on a Sunday, the following day is often observed as the holiday. These are the official holidays, when all government offices and most businesses are closed:

New Year's Day	January 1
Good Friday, Easter Monday	
Victoria Day	Monday before May 24
Canada Day	July 1
Labor Day	1st Monday in September
Thanksgiving	2nd Monday in October
Remembrance Day	November 11 (banks, schools and government offices only)
Christmas	December 25
Boxing Day	December 26
St. Patrick's Day (Newfoundland)	March 17 or the Monday before
St. George's Day (Newfoundland)	April 23 or the Monday before
Discovery Day (Newfoundland)	Monday closest to June 24
Memorial Day (Newfoundland)	Monday closest to July 1
Orangeman's Day (Newfoundland)	Monday before July 12
St-Jean Baptiste (Quebec)	June 24
Civic Holiday (Alberta, British Columbia, Manitoba, New Brunswick, Northwest Territories, Nova Scotia, Ontario, Saskatchewan)	1st Monday in August
Discovery Day (Yukon)	3rd Monday in August

R RADIO AND TELEVISION

You can tune in to the bilingual broadcasts of the CBC (Canadian Broadcasting Corporation), to local offerings or American network television. AM and FM radio stations transmit programmes produced by the CBC and numerous independents, covering the spectrum from rock to jazz and classical music.

TIME ZONES

Canada divides into six zones: Newfoundland (GMT − 3½), Atlantic (GMT − 4), Eastern (GMT − 5), Central (GMT − 6), Mountain (GMT − 7), and Pacific Standard Time (GMT − 8).

Daylight Saving Time is in effect (except in the greater part of Saskatchewan) from April when the clocks go forward an hour until the last Sunday in October, when they revert to standard time.

Pacific	Mountain	Central	Eastern	Atlantic	Nfland	GMT
Vancouver	Edmonton	Winnipeg	**Ottawa**	Halifax	St. John's	London
9 a.m.	10 a.m.	11 a.m.	**noon**	1 p.m.	1.30 p.m.	5 p.m.

TIPPING

In general, service charges are not included in hotel and restaurant bills, and tipping is voluntary. Visitors should keep in mind that the custom of tipping is not as widespread in Canada as it is in the United States and parts of Europe.

Following are a few guidelines:

Airport/hotel porter, per bag	$1
Maid, per day	$2
Waiter	15%
Hairdresser/Barber	10–15%
Taxi driver	10–15%
Tour guide	10%

TOILETS

Canadians will probably understand you whether you ask for the "rest-room", "washroom" or "lavatory". In Quebec, you may encounter the words *Hommes* (Men) and *Dames* (Ladies), though nowadays public conveniences are usually marked with pictographs. Toilets are easily found in service stations, museums, cafés or bars and Métro stations.

TOURIST INFORMATION AGENCIES

Canadian embassies, high commissions and consulates can provide information on travel to Canada.

Provincial tourist offices in Canada:

Numbers with 1-800 in front of them can be called free within North America.

Alberta: Economic Development & Tourism, P.O. Box 2500, Edmonton, Alberta, T5J 2Z4; tel.: 1-800-661-8888.

British Columbia: Tourism British Columbia, Ministry of Tourism, Parliament Buildings, Victoria V8V 1X4; tel.: 1-800-663-6000.

Manitoba: Travel Manitoba, Travel Idea Center, 21 Forks Market Rd., Winnipeg R3C 4T7; tel.: 1-800-665-0040.

New Brunswick: Department of Economic Development and Tourism, P. O. Box 12345, Fredericton E3B 5C3; tel.: 1-800-561-0123.

Newfoundland and Labrador: Department of Tourism and Culture, P.O. Box 8730, St. John's, NF, A1B 4K2; tel.: 1-800-563-6353.

Northwest Territories: TravelArctic, Department of Economic Development and Tourism, Box 1320, Yellowknife, NWT, X1A 2L9; tel.: 1-800-661-0788.

Nova Scotia: Corporatel, 2695 Dutch Village Rd., Suite 501, Halifax, NS, B3J 2R5; tel.: 1-800-565-0000 (from Canada) or 1-800-341-6096 (from the U.S.).

Ontario: 77 Bloor St. West, Toronto, Ontario, N7A 2R9; tel.: 1-800-ONTARIO (668-2746).

Prince Edward Island: Visitor Services Division, Department of Tourism and Parks, P.O. Box 940, Charlottetown C1A 7M5; tel.: 1-800-565-0267.

Quebec: Tourisme Québec, C.P. 979, Montréal, PQ, H3C 2W3; tel.: 1-800-363-7777.

Saskatchewan: Suite 500, 1900 Albert Street, Regina, Saskatchewan, S4P 4L9; tel.: 1-800-667-7191.

Yukon: Tourism Yukon, P.O. Box 2703, Whitehorse Y1A 2C6; tel. 1-800-661-0494 (from Canada, answerphone only): 403 667 5340.

TRANSPORT

By Car (see also DRIVING). Most of the big cities and larger towns lie on or near the Trans-Canada Highway, the country's main east-west artery. It crosses southern Canada from Newfoundland all the way to Victoria on the Pacific, a distance of nearly 8,000 km. The going is slower in the rural north, where roads may be gravel-covered, rather than paved.

Driving Distances. Ottawa–Montreal 203 km, Montreal–Toronto 590 km, Toronto–Halifax 1,854 km, Calgary–Vancouver 1,080 km, Winnipeg–Regina 578 km.

By Air. Air travel is well developed in Canada, with several national and regional companies in operation, as well as dozens of local carriers. Frequent scheduled and charter flights connect the cities and larger towns, while light planes provide regular service to places that are inaccessible by road. Seaplanes shuttle between coastal towns and offshore islands.

By Coach. Greyhound routes cover Canada from coast to coast. And there are numerous regional companies besides, which cooperate to provide convenient country-wide connections. Stopovers may be made on most lines, and passes for cheap travel during specified periods may be available. Greyhound Ameripasses are valid for certain routes into Canada (see p. 230).

By Train. Cross the continent by train (travel time: four days), or take a series of short, scenic journeys—up into the Arctic on the Polar Bear Express, for example. It's essential to book well ahead for these routes during the tourist season. There's just one national company, VIA Rail, the successor to the old Canadian National and Canadian Pacific companies. Several smaller lines operate regional services: the Ontario Northland, Algoma Central and British Columbia railways. Long distance trains are equipped with observation, dining and sleeping cars (with berths, roomettes and bedrooms).

By Boat. Car and passenger ferries shuttle year-round between the mainland and offshore islands. Ferries also serve central Canada's lakes and rivers. Two popular routes are B.C. Ferries' Port Hardy to Prince Rupert run by way of the magnificent Inside Passage, or the spectacular crossing on the Manitoulin Island Ferry from Tobermory to Manitoulin Island in Lake Huron. A replica steamship plys the St. Lawrence River between Kingston and Quebec

City, and the nostalgic *Paddlewheel Queen* and *Paddlewheel Princess* cruise Manitoba's Red River. You can even sail Hudson Bay in season on a tour or charter boat. Icebergs, whales and polar bears complete the scenic attractions.

Local Transport. You'll have no problem getting around the big cities on public transport, be it the underground (subway), bus, tram or trolleybus. The newest thing in Canadian rapid transit is the light railway. Toronto, Edmonton, Calgary and Vancouver, among other cities, have introduced this system.

Subway tickets may be purchased singly or in books, at newsstands or in stations. When you board a city bus in Canada, have the exact fare ready. Drivers never carry change. Ask for a transfer if you have to connect to another line.

Taxis wait for customers at airports, railway stations and hotels. Hail a cab in the street or ask for one by telephone (look in the *Yellow Pages* under "Taxicabs"). A 10–15% tip is customary.

W WEIGHTS AND MEASURES

Canada uses the metric system for most measurements. Road distances and speed are computed in kilometres. The temperature is given in degrees Celsius. Food weights and clothes measurements may be indicated by either the metric system or the American-English one.

Conversion charts

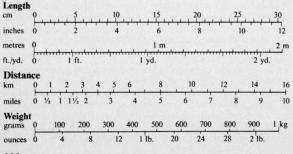

LOWER ONTARIO
AND WESTERN QUEBEC

0   100 km

0   100 miles

J a m e s
B a y

Albany
Kinosheo

Kwetabohigan

Missinaibi
Mattagami

Kesagami L.

Fraserdale

O N T A R I O

Kapuskasing

Kapuskasing

Cochrane

Chapleau

Timmins

Kirkland
Lake

Cobalt

L.
Temagami

hessalon   Sudbury

Espanola

L.
Nipissing

South
Baymouth

Georgian

Tobermory

Bay

Lake
Huron

Owen
Sound

Midland

Barrie

Kitchener   **Toronto**

Stratford
London

Sarnia

Hamilton

troit
ndsor

Lake Erie

L.
Mesgouez

Lac
Mistassini

Lac Evans

Broadback

Matagami

L. au
Goéland

Chibougamau

Q U E B E C

L. Surprise

Lac
Parent

Lac du
Mâle

Réservoir
Gouin

Val-d'Or

Réservoir
Baskatong

N

Trois-Rivières

Ottawa

Pembroke

OTTAWA   **Montreal**

Renfrew

Huntsville

Upper Canada
Village

Orillia

St. Lawrence

Kingston

Lindsay

Thousand
Islands

Oshawa   *Lake*

Mississauga   *Ontario*

U. S.

Niagara

Buffalo

A.

239

Mistassini

North Bay

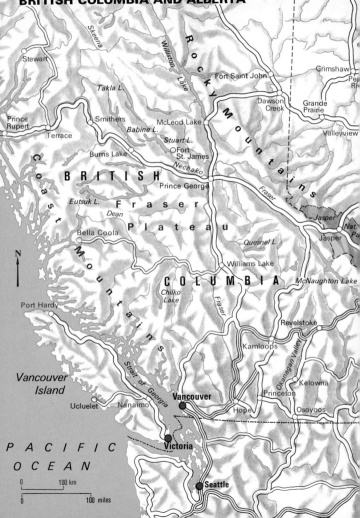

Stewart

Skeena

Williston Lake

Rocky Mountains

Fort Saint John

Grimshaw

Peace River

Takla L.

Dawson Creek

Grande Prairie

Prince Rupert

Smithers

McLeod Lake

Valleyview

Terrace

Babine L.

Stuart L.

Burns Lake

Fort St. James

BRITISH

Nechako

Fraser

Coast

Prince George

Eutsuk L.

Fraser

Jasper

Dean

Plateau

Jasper

Nat Pa

Bella Coola

Quesnel L.

COLUMBIA

Williams Lake

McNaughton Lake

Mountains

Port Hardy

Chilko Lake

Fraser

Revelstoke

Kamloops

Okanagan Valley

Vancouver Island

Strait of Georgia

Kelowna

Ucluelet

Nanaimo

Vancouver

Princeton

Hope

Osoyoos

Victoria

PACIFIC

Seattle

OCEAN

0   100 km

0   100 miles

N

MANITOBA AND UPPER ONTARIO

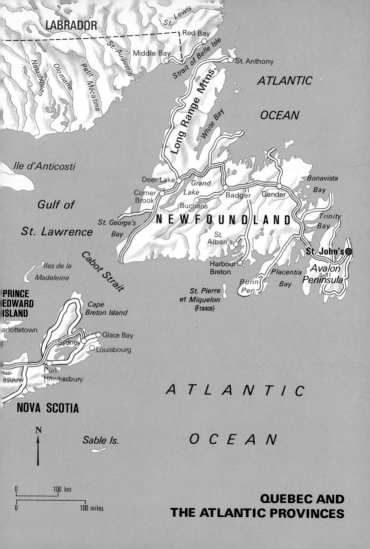

LABRADOR

St. Lewis

Red Bay

Middle Bay

St. Augustin

Strait of Belle Isle

St. Anthony

ATLANTIC

OCEAN

Natashquan

Olomane

petit Mécatina

Long Range Mtns.

White Bay

Ile d'Anticosti

Deer Lake

Grand Lake

Corner Brook

Buchans

Badger

Gander

Bonavista Bay

Gulf of

St. Lawrence

NEWFOUNDLAND

St. George's Bay

St. Alban's

Trinity Bay

St. John's

Iles de la Madeleine

Harbour Breton

Placentia Bay

Avalon Peninsula

Cabot Strait

Burin Pen.

PRINCE EDWARD ISLAND

St. Pierre et Miquelon (France)

arlottetown

Cape Breton Island

Glace Bay

Sydney

Louisbourg

Port Hawkesbury

aswp

NOVA SCOTIA

N

Sable Is.

ATLANTIC

OCEAN

0   100 km

0   100 miles

QUEBEC AND
THE ATLANTIC PROVINCES

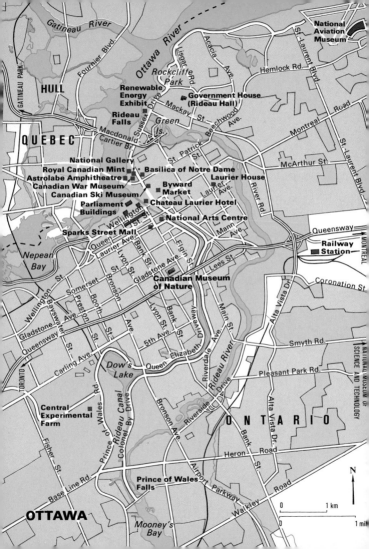

National Aviation
Museum

Gatineau River

Ottawa River

Fournier Blvd.

Usgar St.

Acacia Ave.

Hemlock Rd.

Rockcliffe
Park

St-Laurent Blvd.

GATINEAU PARK

HULL

Renewable
Energy
Exhibit

Government House
(Rideau Hall)

Mackay St.

Montreal

QUEBEC

Rideau
Falls

Macdonald
Cartier Br.

Sussex Drive

Green
Is.

Beechwood Ave.

Road

St-Laurent Blvd.

St. Patrick St.

McArthur St.

National Gallery
Royal Canadian Mint
Astrolabe Amphitheatre
Canadian War Museum
Canadian Ski Museum
Parliament
Buildings

Basilica of Notre Dame
Laurier House
Byward
Market
Chateau Laurier Hotel

Laurier Ave.

River Rd.

Sparks Street Mall

Wellington

National Arts Centre

Queensway

Nepean
Bay

Queen St.

Laurier Ave.

Bank St.

Elgin St.

Mann Ave.

Railway
Station

MONTREAL

Wellington St.

Bayswater Ave.

Somerset St.

Preston St.

Bronson Ave.

Lyon St.

Gladstone Ave.

Lees St.

Canadian Museum
of Nature

Coronation St.

Gladstone St.

Queensway

Booth St.

Lyon St.

5th Ave.

Bank St.

Driveway

Main St.

Alta Vista Dr.

Smyth Rd.

Carling Ave.

Dow's
Lake

Queen Elizabeth

Riverdale Ave.

Rideau River

Riverside Drive

Pleasant Park Rd.

Alta Vista Dr.

TORONTO

Central
Experimental
Farm

Rideau Canal
Colonel By Drive

Prince of Wales Rd.

Bronson Ave.

Riverside

O N T A R I O

Heron

Bank St.

Road

A NATIONAL MUSEUM OF SCIENCE AND TECHNOLOGY

Fisher St.

Base Line Rd.

Prince of Wales
Falls

Airport Parkway

Walkley Rd.

Road

N

OTTAWA

Mooney's
Bay

0   1 km

0   1 mil

TORONTO—DOWNTOWN

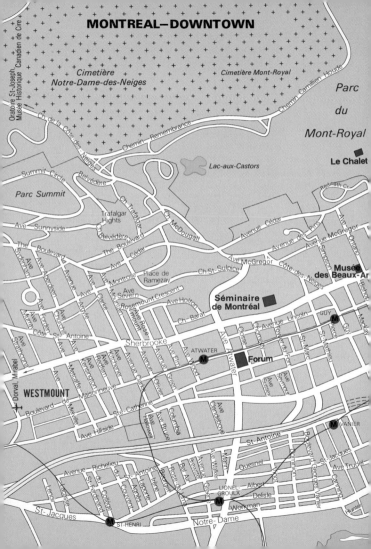

QUEBEC CITY -
MIDTOWN

Bassin Louise

St-Laurent

Citadelle

Le Grand Théâtre

Manège Militaire

Parc des Champs de Bataille

Plaines d'Abraham

Château Frontenac

Couvent des Ursulines

Assemblée Nationale

Hôtel des Postes

Hôtel Dieu

Séminaire de Québec

Basilique Notre-Dame

Musée du Fort

Monument de Champlain

Maison Chevalier

Église Notre-Dame-des-Victoires

Maison Cremazie

Maison Touchet

Monument de Jacques-Cartier

Porte St-Louis

N

0   100   200   300 m

INDEX

An asterisk (*) next to a page number indicates a map reference. Where there is more than one set of page references, the one in bold type refers to the main entry. For index to Practical Information, see pages 218-9.